S0-BDL-411

Come Holy Spirit
help us to pray

Benedict M. Heron OSB

Foreword by
Bishop Ambrose Griffiths OSB

New Life Publishing
Luton

First published in 2000 by
New Life Publishing
60 Wickstead Avenue
Luton Beds. LU4 9DP

© 2000 Benedict M. Heron OSB

British Library Cataloguing in Publication Data
A catalogue record for this book is available
from the British Library

All rights reserved. No part of this book may be
reproduced , stored in a retrieval system, or transmitted
by any means - electronic, mechanical, photocopying,
recording, or otherwise without the prior written
permission of the publishers.

ISBN   0 9529159 8 7

Scripture quotations are taken from the Revised Standard Version of
the Bible, copyright 1946, 1952 and 1971 by the Division of Christian
Education of the National Council of the Churches of Christ, U.S.A.

Cover design by Yvonne Bell, 02380 773271. Yvonne creates Stoles,
Chasubles and Copes to individual designs, often on silk - as for
the cover of this book. She paints icons, Celtic motifs and Medieval
illuminations; makes church banners, designs Christmas cards and
illustrates the Gospel message.

Typesetting by New Life Publishing, Luton
Printed and Bound in Great Britain by
Biddles Limited, Guildford, Surrey.

Contents

This book is dedicated to the many
kind people who have supported
the writing of it with their prayers.
Without their prayers it would certainly
never have been written.

Acknowledgements

There are many people I need and want to thank in connection with the writing of this book. I thank Bishop Ambrose Griffiths, OSB for his very kind Foreword and Charles Whitehead, President of the International Catholic Charismatic Renewal Council, for a not less kind notice on the back cover.

Very warm thanks are due to my publishers, Gerard and Toni Pomfret of New Life Publishing, who could not have been more helpful and encouraging in every way. They also made valuable suggestions for improving what I had written.

Special thanks are due to Joan Lewington, who patiently deciphered my difficult handwriting and typed the text, as well as rendering help in many other ways.

My sister, Joanna Gent, and my brother Giles provided peaceful and welcoming homes in beautiful surroundings to which I escaped at times to get on with the writing, free from other calls on time and energy. My brother also tidied up my style and helpfully challenged some of the things I had written.

Talks with Father Augustine Hoey on prayer, helped me to clarify my thoughts and provided encouragement. Peter Tyler successfully helped me to overcome my hesitations in connection with the chapter on Listening to God. I also found valuable their writings on prayer. To these two people and to so many others who have shared with me about their life of prayer, I must give thanks.

Many thanks are also due to my monastic community, who have allowed me the freedom to develop my healing ministry, and have supported me in many other ways.

I also want to thank everyone at Holy Trinity, Brompton and the Alpha course. Their vibrant faith and ecumenical openness have been a source of inspiration to me.

Finally, a very big thanks to all those kind people who prayed for the writing of this book. I have been aware of being upheld by their prayers. In a very real sense the book is not my book but our book. It is only when, by the grace of God, we get to heaven, we shall fully know how much we owe to the prayers of others.

Dom Benedict Heron, OSB   January 2000

Foreword

At a time of crisis in the Church we naturally ask where we are going wrong. Various solutions are proposed but they all have one thing in common. Unless they are supported by sincere and persevering prayer they will never renew the Church. We need to recover our confidence in the value and effectiveness of prayer and give it a much higher priority in our lives.

I remember once listening to a sermon which emphasised how hard it was to pray and I felt thoroughly depressed. I had the opposite experience when I first attended a prayer group and heard other people praying. Only then did I realise that prayer could be joyful and full of praise and thanksgiving. As you read this book you will enjoy a similar gift as Father Benedict Heron shares with us so much of his personal experience. He avoids the assumptions and theory of other treatments and writes in easy everyday language with an almost conversational style. He has the knack of bringing out familiar phrases like "Thy will be done" in their full and very demanding import. And just when we think we could never emulate him, he admits his own shortcomings with disarming honesty.

Everyone must pray as they can, and not force themselves into a particular mould, but certain threads are common to all prayer. We are unlikely to progress very far unless we make a serious attempt to listen to God as well as speaking to Him. Many find this difficult but chapter five gives a convincing and balanced treatment illustrated with personal anecdotes. Intercession is vital for the renewal of the Church and many other needs, but an effectiveness depends on our faith and persevering commitment. All prayer is hampered by a failure to repent of our sins and a lack of awareness of the false gods and collective sins characteristic of society today. If instead of being aware of these evils, we are undiscerning and indulgent in our selection of television, films, and books, we will face great obstacles when we come to pray.

There is a wealth of encouragement and guidance for everyone in this book. In order to make it accessible to all certain aspects of prayer which are less generally applicable have been treated in an appendix. But what we will all carry away with us is a deep conviction of the importance of prayer and a realisation that this is the key to the future growth of the Church.

Bishop Ambrose Griffiths   January 2000

Introduction

Let me start by trying to say what this book seeks to do and what it does not. This book is not a learned study on prayer. I would not be the right person to do that. Nor does this book seek to cover every aspect of prayer. There will be gaps. There is also a fuller treatment of the prayer of intercession. This book seeks, God willing, to help those who read it to pray better. If it does that I will be more than satisfied.

I had given a series of seven talks on prayer to our Cockfosters ecumenical prayer group. Some of those present kindly said they had found the talks helpful and encouraged me to try to turn the talks into a book, and my publisher, New Life Publishing, also kindly encouraged me to do so. So the seven talks form the basis of the book, although there have been a considerable number of additions in the process of writing.

Prayer is a glorious adventure. It is not always easy, indeed there can, normally will be, desert or difficult periods at times. Prayer is for me a joyful struggle. At times the joyful aspect dominates, at the other times it is largely a struggle. However, the adventure of prayer is always immensely and wonderfully worthwhile.

Prayer is not the most important thing in the Christian life. The primacy belongs to love, as St Paul reminds us in I Corinthians 13. The two great commandments of Jesus are about love: "And he said to him, 'You shall love the Lord your God with all your heart, and with all your soul, and with all your mind'. This is the great and first commandment. And a second is like it, 'You shall love your neighbour as yourself. On these two commandments depend all the law and the prophets'."

St John of the Cross, quoted in the Catechism *(1022)*, says that "at the evening of life, we shall be judged on our love." The division between the sheep and the goats in Matthew 25 is based on love of the neighbour. "Before him will be gathered all the nations, and he will separate them one from another as a shepherd separates the sheep from the goats, and he will place the sheep at his right hand, but the goats on his left" *(Matthew 25: 32-33)*. However, there is normally a very close connection between love and prayer. For many Christians growth in prayer is of fundamental importance for growth in love of God and love of our neighbour.

Nevertheless, Jesus also stressed the importance of prayer: "Then Jesus told them a parable to pray always and not to lose heart" *(Luke 18:1)*; He frequently went aside to pray on his own: "In those days he went out into the hills to pray: and all night he continued to pray to God" *(Luke 6:12)*; and He prayed in Gethsemanie and on the Cross. For many Christians growth in prayer will be the royal road to growth in love. In Great Britain, as in most of the First World, the number of people who are regularly attending worship in a Christian Church is in general declining, sometimes quickly, and the relative absence of the younger generation in many churches is normally only too obvious. Numbers is not everything, but this decline in numbers is accompanied by a decrease of Christian influence on the population as a whole, which is increasingly influenced by materialism, secularist standards, violence, and sexual laxity. Surely every Christian should be deeply concerned by what is happening.

It is my conviction that the neglect of prayer is largely responsible for the spiritual weakness of many Christians, the tepidity of many Christian groups, the declining numbers in so many churches, and the ineffectiveness of much Christian witness and outreach. Indeed, I would say that there is a widespread crisis of confidence in the value and effectiveness of prayer among many Christians. Hence my efforts in this book to encourage the practice of prayer, and hopefully to help people to pray or pray better. I believe that the task I am seeking to undertake is of absolutely vital importance for the Church today, however small may be my contribution to it.

I write as someone who has been a monk since 1946, a Catholic priest since 1954, and I have been deeply involved in prayer groups since 1972. None of the above makes any sense at all if you do not have real confidence in the value of prayer. I pray that the Holy Spirit will use this book, despite my limitations, to encourage and help others to pray - and indeed to share my enthusiasm for the glorious, if sometimes difficult, adventure of prayer.

I am a Roman Catholic, but in my life of prayer I have been helped not only by Catholics, but also by contacts with and the writings of Anglicans, the Orthodox, Quakers, Pentecostals and other Christians. The life of prayer transcends denominational barriers. So I hope that this book will be of help not only to some Catholics, but also to other Christians, and that it will make a small contribution to the desire of Jesus "that they may all be one".

Chapter One
The Holy Spirit, Our Spiritual Director

When and How Should we Pray?

The short answer and the final answer to that question is when and how the Holy Spirit leads us. Authentic prayer is the work of the Holy Spirit within us, although of course we have to co-operate with the Holy Spirit. So if I deliberately decide without due reason to watch a soap opera on television instead of going to Church on Sunday, then I cannot blame the Holy Spirit.

It needs to be said that the Holy Sprit will guide no two people's life of prayer in exactly the same way, for we are all unique people with a unique relationship with God. Moreover the Holy Spirit will not guide someone in prayer in exactly the same way this year as last year. We have an ongoing and developing relationship with God.

God wants us to live in a Christian community, not as isolated individuals on our own. So the Holy Spirit's guidance in prayer will take into account the communal aspect and setting of our life of prayer. Thus, for example, the Holy Spirit will normally guide Catholics to go to Mass on Sunday, following the practice and discipline of their church.

The Holy Spirit should be our Spiritual Director, although of course it can be, and normally is, helpful to have a human spiritual counsellor with whom we can share. Thus much that I write in this book should be

1

seen as hints about the life of prayer, to be accepted or left aside as the Holy Spirit guides and as it is found helpful or not. Obviously it is good to be in touch with the wide Christian tradition of prayer and spiritual life, for the Holy Spirit guides many people in much the same way and the Holy Spirit also guides to some extent through the wisdom and experience of other people. However, in the end our personal relationship with God is fundamental.

A former Abbot of Downside, Abbot Chapman, used to say: "Pray as you can, and not as you can't". I think that there is a great wisdom in that advice. Do we not all find that certain ways of praying help us and others do not? That if we try to pray in one way it flows and that if we try in another way we are 'blocked'! So, for example, there is nothing to be gained by following advice to pray the 'Jesus prayer' for half an hour each morning if all that happens is that we become irritable, discouraged, or fall asleep. If we find ourselves "blocked" when we try to pray in a certain way that is normally a sign that the Holy Spirit does not want us to pray in that way, at least for the time being.

So may I ask you, reader, to accompany your reading of this book with prayer to the Holy Spirit, so that your Spiritual Director may show you what at this time is for you, and what is not and perhaps never will be.

Come Holy Spirit!

Chapter Two
Time Given to Prayer

"Then Jesus told them a parable about their need to pray always and not to lose heart "(*John 18.1*). St Paul tells us "to pray without ceasing". (*I Thess 5. 17*). Does this mean that we should always be saying prayers? I think not. If the surgeon was repeating the Our Father throughout the operation, the operation would probably go wrong. I think that the instructions of Jesus and St Paul are a call to move towards a contemplative living in the presence of Jesus or God such as we find in the lives of many mystics and saints, not a call to be saying prayers all the time. For example, St Teresa of Avila and Brother Lawrence, the author of "The Practice of the Presence of God", remained closely united to God in contemplative prayer in the midst of intense activity. That would also be true of many other saints.

However, if most of us are to move towards a contemplative living in the presence of God, we need to set aside sufficient time to give to prayer on its own, not just praying while we are doing the ironing or driving through London. We need to set aside time to concentrate on prayer.

Now comes the crunch question: How much time should we normally set apart for prayer daily, weekly? Obviously, the right answer to this question will vary enormously according to our personality, our vocation and our circumstances. A new Christian who has only just started praying may find a quarter of an hour per day right, while this would be totally inadequate for a monk or pastor. A busy mother with a job may not be able to set aside much time daily for prayer, but of course Jesus will fully understand this and He will bless her life of prayer if she does what she can. An invalid lying in bed all day may well be called to spend hours a day praying; this could be her or his special form of service and ministry, it may be the occupation which gives meaning to her or his life.

Nevertheless, I want to suggest that the time given to prayer by most Christians in our country, and in many other countries, is woefully inadequate, and that this goes a considerable way towards explaining why in general our numbers and influence are seriously declining and why we have largely lost the younger generation. A Christianity which has to a considerable extent lost contact with Jesus, with God, through lack of prayer is a dying Christianity - and that is what we can often see around us.

By contrast, in those places where there are fervent praying congregations, we often see expanding, sometimes rapidly expanding, churches, for example in London Holy Trinity, Brompton and Kensington Temple. In the capital of South Korea, Seoul, there is the Pentecostal congregation founded by Dr Cho which has 750,000 members. Dr Cho tells his congregation that he expects them normally to spend between one and two hours in prayer every morning before they go to work, and his church has acquired a mountain to which many members of the church go for prayer and fasting, normally for three days. On the Catholic side, there is a charismatic community in Manila in the Philippines which arranges a weekly all-night vigil of prayer which is attended by about a million people.

I am not suggesting that one can automatically transfer what is happening in South Korea or in the Philippines to London or Paris. I am suggesting, however, that what is happening in those places should give us a powerful and salutary shock over the question of prayer, the time we give to it, and the importance we attach to it.

Let us face it. Many Christians who go to church on Sunday will only give about five minutes to their daily prayer, and those who do not normally go to church on Sunday may well say no prayers most days. How can we hope to maintain a living relationship with Jesus, with God, based on only five minutes regular daily prayer? The average person in this country, we are told, spends 27 hours per week looking at television, so much of which is worldly tripe. Which is going to win, the long hours of television or the few minutes of prayer? No wonder that moral standards decline, while drug abuse, sexual immorality, violence, selfishness, greed and dishonesty increase.

Delia Smith, the well-known cook, was suggesting for Catholics, Mass plus one hour's personal prayer daily. Obviously not everyone can get to Mass daily, but her suggestion surely shows us the sort of way in which we should be thinking. St Francis of Assisi said that it sometimes took him an hour to get through to God in prayer, no wonder that so many five-minuters never really get through to God.

When we say the Our Father we say "Thy will be done on earth as it is in heaven". If we really mean what we say, we are telling God that we want to spend as much time (not more) in prayer as He wants. I think that many of us need to examine our use of time and energy. How much time do I spend each week looking at TV, listening to the radio, reading newspapers etc. and how much time do I spend in spiritual reading of the Bible and other spiritual books and praying? Have I got my priorities right, am I using my time and energy as God wants?

Do not misunderstand me. I am not against all television, radio and newspapers. We need to keep in touch - there are some excellent television and radio programmes, and we do need some relaxation. But have we got the balance right? Very often, surely the truthful answer is "No". I often meet people who tell me how their prayer life has deepened considerably since they got rid of the television set - although not everyone is called to do that.

Some people will say that they do not have a regular time of prayer, but pray when they feel like it. I think that experience teaches many of us that if we only pray when we feel like it we normally do not do much praying - the devil sees to it that we do not very often feel like praying. Of course it is an excellent thing to pray when we feel like it, *but not only then.*

A serious life of prayer normally requires that we set aside an adequate amount of time daily to give to prayer, which we do not drop unless there is a real reason for doing so. We need if possible to choose a time when we are not too tired and are less likely to be interrupted. For most people that will probably mean the early morning, and it may often involve getting up half an hour or more earlier. For some people last thing at night may be the best time for prayer, I think that every Christian will surely want to start and end the day with prayer, but I am not alone in finding that if I try to prolong my prayer before going to bed I frequently drop off to sleep in a chair. Ask God to guide you in your choice of prayer times and to give you the strength to be disciplined - but not too rigid. When love is really calling us to do something else we should drop or shorten our prayer time without scruples or hesitation. Our spiritual life will not suffer if we drop or shorten our prayer time at the call of God but it will suffer if we drop it or shorten it for the wrong reasons.

Sometimes we may need longer periods of prayer than is possible in our daily routine. Perhaps once a week or once a month we should set aside a longer period of prayer. Once when I was following a spiritual directors course in another monastery, I was often able to spend two hours in prayer in the afternoon, and I found that two hours was, so to speak, more than twice one hour - I seemed to go quite a bit deeper.

A number of people come to our and other monasteries for a retreat for a few days or even just one day of recollection. These longer periods of prayer are proving a real blessing for so many people.

I notice on re-reading this section I have said nothing about prayer vigils at night - perhaps because I have never been good at staying up praying through the night! When I last visited Holy Trinity at Brompton they were announcing a prayer vigil from 10.00 p.m. to 6.00 a.m. in the morning, and the Benedictine nuns of Tyburn in London organise regular prayer vigils through the night.

Obviously these prayer vigils can be very helpful times of prayer, but do not feel upset or guilty if you like me are someone who would just drop off to sleep and disturb the others with your snoring! Not everything is for everyone.

I can imagine some readers of this section saying to themselves that this monk has not a clue what life in the real world is like. Many people, they will say, have to face so many calls on time and energy that all talk of longer daily prayer sessions is totally unrealistic. To which I reply that I know quite a number of busy people working in the world who manage to spend over an hour a day praying. I think of a medical doctor with a regular job who used to get up at about 5.00 am to have enough time to pray at length before going to work. Of course, I do not expect everyone to be able to do that. But if some people can do that, perhaps others could increase considerably their hurried five minutes.

There is a further consideration. Increasing the time given to prayer often increases the quality of activity, indeed our activity can gain much more in quality than it may lose in quantity. And often it will not lose in quantity because being more Spirit led we shall go down fewer blind alleys and make fewer mistakes. I know two priests who independently, when some years ago they were faced with mounting demands on time and energy, responded by doubling the hour they were accustomed to spend daily in private personal prayer: they felt that was the only way in which they could fruitfully cope with the increased demands and pressures.

At the end of this section I simply ask the reader to

pray about what I have written, to see whether there is anything in it for you. I know that people can use prayer as an excuse for avoiding unwelcome activity, and I know of course that some people are by temperament and vocation more Marthas than Marys. I thank God for the Marthas, and for all the ways in which I personally have been helped by them. I will end this chapter by repeating the quotation of St John of the Cross: "At the evening of this life, we shall be judged on our love" - not on the amount of time we have spent praying. But more praying will frequently result in more love, indeed sometimes in very much more love.

Chapter Three
Repentance

Our daily prayer should surely normally include repentance, offering, listening, asking and praising, not necessarily in that order. I think it can often be good to start and end with praise. So the following chapters will be on these aspects of prayer.

We all need to repent, for we are all sinners. We all need to say frequently with the tax collector in the Gospel, "God be merciful to me a sinner" *(Luke 18:13)*. In this life we shall never be so holy that we no longer need to repent. At the beginning of the Mass there is a prayer of repentance for everyone. Indeed, if anyone thinks they do not need to repent, they have a special need to repent of spiritual pride.

The special saints usually have a greater spirit of repentance than the rest of us. Being nearer to Jesus than we are, they can see more clearly than we the spiritual things in their lives which are not like the life of Jesus, the failings which are not in line with the teachings of Jesus. So we are all called not only to go on repenting, but also to go on growing in the grace and virtue of repentance.

As the years go by, I find new areas in my life where repentance is needed. I do not think I am more sinful than I used to be - thanks to the grace of God and the prayers of other people. But I am more aware of certain areas of my life where I need to repent, I am also sure that there are still further areas awaiting repentance when I am ready. I think that sin goes so deep in each of us, that it is normally only little by little that we are able to face up to the necessity of repentance. For example, in my own life it is only in recent times that I am becoming more aware of my exaggerated self-centredness, which cannot just be psychologically explained away - sin is involved. There is pride and selfishness there. Jesus said: "Be perfect, therefore, as your heavenly Father is perfect" *(Matthew 5:48)*. So we need not worry that we shall run out of things for which we need to repent!

Some sins are fairly obvious, although it is surprising how successful we can be in explaining them away, in justifying our sinfulness. Adultery can be seen as kindness to another person. Stealing can be seen as restoring justice. Cruelty can be seen as teaching someone a necessary lesson. Pride can be seen as a rightful self-respect. Racism can be seen as loyalty to one's country. Alcohol abuse can be seen as necessary relaxation. Jealousy and envy can be seen as promoting truth. Laziness can be seen as a due regard for one's health. Greed can be seen as a just reward. Unforgiveness can be seen as not being soft. Lack of trust can be seen as prudent realism. The list could go on. Our minds can be wonderfully fertile when it comes to not recognising our sinfulness!

Let us, for example, look at our failures in not trusting God enough, which involves lack of faith and hope. In the picture of Jesus connected with the devotion to the Divine Mercy there are the words, "Jesus I trust in You". When I pray before that picture I am often painfully aware in how many areas I am not trusting Jesus: for example, questions of health, shortage of time and energy, relationships, my priestly ministry, intercessory prayer, the future. In the uncertainties of today's world, when there is often very little job security, when so many marriages are breaking up, when violence is on the increase, when children are getting involved with drugs, when so many people are living under pressure, there is often a great need to trust God. And if that is true for people living in England, what about those living in say many parts of Africa, where there is much less security at the human level?

So what do we do about our failure to trust God? I frequently need to repent of my lack of faith and hope, my failure to trust Jesus, and then I ask God for greater gifts of faith and hope. Then I try to step out in faith, however I am feeling.

Another area where many people need to repent is that of lack of love, charity - indeed, we surely all need to repent of our failing in love, and not infrequently, I quite often have to battle with feelings of wrong anger, indeed sometimes with thoughts of violence. The devil, playing on our weak spots, can put such thoughts in our minds. Repentance is part of the way of fighting such thoughts.

Lack of love can take so many forms, from the violence we read about in the newspapers to unloving thoughts and sins of omission. In one sense every sin is an expression of lack of love. If we loved God and our neighbour more there would be less injustices, jealousy, envy, greed, lust, laziness and all the other sins.

Our lack of love can be focused on this or that individual person or on a group. Some people tend to be angry and unloving towards members of the opposite sex. Some people focus their hatred on members of other races. One has only to think of the utterly appalling hatred which Christians have so often had for the Jews down the centuries! How right Pope John Paul II is to publicly repent of our sins in this area.

Unforgiveness is a very common expression of lack of love. Jesus taught us to pray: "Forgive us our trespasses as we forgive those who trespass against us". As a priest I find that many of the people who come to me for help are struggling with a problem of forgiveness - indeed at times I am having to struggle myself! And some of the people who come to me are not struggling with this problem but ought to be. They have not yet faced up to the demands of the Christian gospel on this point.

When people have been very badly hurt by others in life, it is very understandable that they cannot easily forgive. Indeed, without a special grace from God they will not succeed in doing so. Think, for example, of the faithful wife whose husband has left her penniless with four young children to join up with another younger woman; or there is the person who has in old age been cheated of all their life's savings; or the person who has been deliberately blinded by muggers in order to take their handbag or wallet; or the priest who has been falsely accused of sexual misbehaviour. In all these cases someone's life can feel as if it has totally collapsed at the human level. The last thing they feel like is forgiving!

Yet even in circumstances like these we have to seek to follow the command of Jesus to forgive, and this means repenting of all unforgiveness and asking God for the grace to forgive. People will reply sometimes that they have tried to forgive but the unforgiving feelings simply keep coming up and overwhelming them. Yes, we cannot always control our feelings. But forgiveness is primarily a question of the will, not the feelings. So we can by the grace of God make an act of the will, forgiving and asking Jesus also to forgive the person who has wronged us, and praying for the offender: "But I say to you, love your enemies and pray for those who persecute you" *(Matthew 5:43)*. (It may help us to forgive in difficult circumstances if we remember that we are the first victims of our own unforgiveness).

Finally, in the matter of repenting of our lack of love, sometimes sins of omissions are the area where repentance is most needed. The support and help we have not given, the financial aid we have withheld when we could easily have given, the prayers we have not said, our lack of concern for our neighbour. Without becoming scrupulous, it can sometimes be good to examine our conscience on these omissions. And this can include our failure to praise and thank God which shows a lack of love.

Following Ezekiel *(Chapter 36)*, we can repent of our "heart of stone" and ask God to find us "a new heart", "a heart of flesh".

Pride is another area where there is often much need for repentance. Once again, we all need to repent of our pride at times. Our pride can take so many forms, we can be proud in so many areas of our lives, and the devil is clever at hiding our pride from us. I find it difficult to know what to say when someone who has come to me for spiritual help solemnly assures me that they are a humble person and never have any trouble with pride. I feel like saying: "That is wonderful. I will write to the Vatican and arrange for your immediate canonisation". What I actually say is: "Perhaps there is some area of your life where you are not perfectly humble, and where therefore perhaps there is sometimes at least a little pride". Not many people are willing to say that they are always perfectly humble in every way! That can be the way in.

Yes, we can be proud of so many things. Our good looks - that has never been for me a particular source of temptation! (St Francis de Sales, so I am told, once replied to a woman who confessed that she spent too much time admiring her beauty in a mirror, that in her case that was primarily a matter of mistaken judgement). We can be proud of our family, our ancestry, our class, our relationships (I tend to name drop). I knew a woman now dead who was completely cut off by her family because she married beneath her, she married a man who was a mere medical doctor.

We can be proud of our possessions, money, career and income. Why drive around in a car costing £150,000 when a car costing so much less would be more than adequate? Surely the reason is largely so that other people may know you can afford such a car. It is not only the very wealthy who can have problems of that kind. There can be a one-upmanship in possessions right down to the very poor.

Then there are the many forms of intellectual and cultural pride. In some circles you can be made to feel rather out of it if you do not know about the philosophy of Sartre, or the music of Beethoven, or the paintings of Cezanne, or the poetry of T.S. Eliot, or the novels of

Tolkien. People without university degrees can also be regarded as somewhat second class in academic circles.

There can be pride connected with sport and athletics. Some people spend much time and energy in keeping their muscles bulging, their golf handicap down, and in seeking to play for their county or town, in rugby or soccer, or snooker. How proud I was when I was first selected to play for my school's first fifteen in rugby!

Then there is masculine pride. If one looks at the long history of humanity, the normal thing has usually been for women to be largely regarded as second class human beings, to be dominated and pushed around by men. Thank God that has largely changed in some places, but many men still need to repent of the pride present in their attitudes towards women. Not a few men still find it difficult to work under the authority of a woman, however much the woman is the right person to be in the position of authority. However, the right solution is not to go to the opposite extreme of feminine superiority, which is sometimes happening today in certain circles.

Finally, there is spiritual pride and clerical pride. We can look down on people who have not read St Teresa, or who do not know what the divine office is, or who have never heard of Fatima, or who do not pray with the gift of tongues, or who have no Bible, or do not know where to find the letter of St James in the New Testament, or who do not know what a novena is, or who have never heard of Billy Graham or Mother Teresa. We can also look down on people who are single parents, or who have an alcoholic problem, or who have an addiction to gambling, or who have been in prison for theft, or who do not know what man is the father of their child, or who have a homosexual orientation.

As to clerical pride, the clergy can easily feel they have got somewhere when they are ordained and can walk about in a clerical collar. It is not always good for the humility of the clergy when people treat them with exaggerated deference and tell them how very wonderful all their sermons are. Clerical pride causes much harm in some parishes where the clerical leader insists on taking nearly all important decisions on his own and fails to make use of the laity's gifts and experience. I personally have needed at times to repent of my clerical pride. There have been occasions when I have made some lay people feel that they were rather second class Christians.

So it should not be difficult to see that we at times need to repent of our pride. Ask the Holy Spirit to show you when and where you are being called to repent in this way, to give you the grace to do so at an ever deeper level. And ask the Holy Spirit to give you an ever greater gift of joyful authentic humility.

I write 'authentic' humility because we do not want false humility, Authentic humility is based on truth. So, if God has given you an artistic or musical gift, do not deny it, but recognise it, use it and thank God for it. If God has used you to do something for His Kingdom, do not pretend that He has not. But thank Him and give Him the glory.

I do not think that in general people should seek humiliations in order to grow in humility. However, because pride goes so deep in each one of us, I do not think that most people will grow all that much in humility unless they experience humiliations.

Humiliations do not automatically lead to humility - they can turn people to drink or drugs or suicide. But humiliations are always a call and opportunity to grow in humility. So let us seek to use our humiliations in life positively. Things like physical handicaps, inability to pass exams, being unable to find a job or a spouse, being made redundant, the breaking up of a marriage, one's children taking to drugs, being falsely accused of a crime, becoming physically dependent on others through, for example, blindness, becoming incontinent or senile, can all be turned through the grace of God into greater humility. In all such situations pride will normally to some extent be present in our reactions and frustrations. Repentance for pride will be part of the true way forward of letting God bring good out of evil, of growing in holiness.

There is no space here for going into all the other areas of sinfulness which call for repentance. However, it is, I think, right to mention the importance of persevering in repentance. By this I do not mean going on repenting endlessly for sins that have been forgiven. That can often be spiritually unhealthy, it can show a lack of faith in God's forgiveness. What I mean is that we can easily become discouraged when we have gone on repenting for a particular sin and yet have continued to go on repeating that sin. It may, for example, be a sin of alcohol abuse or a sexual sin like indulging in pornography or visiting prostitutes. Having tried to give up the habit, perhaps even for a long time, and failed, people can easily come to the conclusion that they are a hopeless case and there is no point in repenting and trying any more. "Love .... hopes all things (1

Corinthians 13)." Without becoming obsessed by the problems, they should never give up repenting and trying to overcome the difficulty. There are many people who have been gloriously liberated from a habitual sin after years of trying, and their lives have been wonderfully transformed.

Then there is the question of collective sin and repentance. I mentioned earlier the absolutely horrific way in which Christians so often treated Jews for many centuries. One could mention also England's treatment of Ireland in the past, and the slave trade in which vast numbers of Africans were shipped to America. There are many other examples in history. Even though we may not have personally sinned in such cases, yet we have a certain human solidarity with the past and present of our own people, and it is right that we should repent and tell God and other people that we are sorry for these sins, that we apologise to God and other people for them.

Obviously collective repentance for the past or present is something very different from repenting of our own personal sins. When we meet Jesus after this life, we shall have to answer for our own personal sins and not those of our ancestors or contemporaries. But we are right to feel sorry for these collective sins, past or present, and to tell God and others so, and to make amends when possible or appropriate.

Repentance can be regarded as something rather negative and grim. Let us, some Christians may think, concentrate uniquely on joyful praise and thanksgiving, on the positive side of things. But we cannot cut out repentance - not until we get to heaven. *There is no authentic, joyful praise unless we have been through repentance.*

Sometimes in a prayer meeting we are trying to praise joyfully, but somehow it is not authentic. But if we turn to true repentance and then return to praise, the praise will really be joyful and take off. The same applies at the individual level. My praise and thanksgiving will be largely dead if what God is calling me to do at this moment is to repent.

Something similar can be said about the sacrament of reconciliation or confession. It is basically a truly joyful, cleansing, healing sacrament, not a negative concentration on guilt and sin. At times this sacrament can be used by Jesus to lift heavy burdens of guilt and sin off people's backs. At other times it can be rather like taking a bath when you are beginning to feel sticky - we emerge feeling cleaner and more joyful. I personally find that confession more or less monthly is for me a source of grace and makes me feel better, happier, and more peaceful. I am not saying that everyone should go to confession monthly, but I do think that many people who have more or less dropped this sacrament have spiritually lost something by doing so. I also think that confessing one's sins to another individual can have spiritual advantages at the level of humility and guidance - I note that many evangelicals who would not talk about confession as a sacrament nevertheless encourage this individual sharing.

So we should see the gift of repentance as a truly liberating, healing, cleansing, joyful grace, without which we will not grow as we should in true fruitfulness and holiness in our lives. We should ask God for a true and greater gift of repentance, ask the Holy Spirit to show us where we need to repent and to give us the grace to do so.

Then there is the need for collective repentance in our society and our world. There are so many things going on in our country and our world which are an abomination to God. War, violence, terrorism, torture, cruelty, oppression, slavery, persecution, murder, the killing of the innocent by abortion, the sexual abuse of children, sexual immorality in general, great luxury alongside destitution and starvation, economic injustice and exploitation, the rape of the environment, gross cruelty to animals, the list could go on. Surely we Christians should be repenting not only on our own behalf but also in a sense on behalf of humanity as a whole. Let us remember the words of 2 Chronicles 7:14: "If my people who are called by my name humble themselves pray, seek my face, and turn from their wicked ways, then I will hear from heaven, and will forgive their sin and heal their land." It is not only the Christians who will be healed, but also our 'land'.

We Christians have the task not only of repenting for our own sins, but also in a sense of repenting for the world around us and for the many people who have little or no understanding of what true repentance is about. Like Moses we can repent and plead for God's erring children.

Obviously, repenting for the sins of the world and apologising to God for them is something different from repenting for our own personal sins. At the end of this life I shall have to answer to God for my own sins but not those of other people. However, because of our human solidarity with others it is right that we tell God how sorry we are for their sins. For example, if Himmler, who played an important role in the murder of six million Jews, had been my father, surely I would be right to apologise to God for his sins, to be deeply sorry about them, and to tell God so. The same could be said about England's past treatment of Ireland.

When Jesus started preaching, he said, "Repent, and believe in the gospel" *(Mark 11:5)*. He is still saying that to each of us today. Let us get on with it: we will find it is the way to true healing, fruitfulness, peace and joy.

Chapter Four
Offering

"Thy will be done on earth as it is in heaven" *(Matthew 6:9)*. We probably say the Our Father fairly frequently, but how far do we really mean it, how far do I mean it? Because if I fully mean it I am asking that God's perfect will may be done in me always, and in everything connected with me. Not God's second best, tenth best, hundredth best, but his perfect will in every aspect of my life. Of course nothing happens in this world which God does not permit, but we are not talking here about God's permissive will - he permitted Hitler to kill six million Jews - but about God's perfect will. (God did not want Hitler to kill the Jews but He allowed it to happen).

So when I pray "Thy will be done on earth as it is in heaven" I am saying to God, if I truly mean it: "My bank account is yours, my car, my house, my books, my jewellery. I am only your steward. Tell me what you want me to do with my property and give me the grace to do it". The same applies to my time, my energy, my marriage, my family, my relationships, my sexuality, my job, my talents, my opportunities, my health, my present, and my future. I have to hand over everything to God, to Jesus, including my sinfulness, weakness, and brokenness, for I cannot cope with these on my own without the help and grace and mercy of Jesus.

At times there has been a tendency among some Catholics to think that the clergy, the religious and a few other devout people are called to seek perfection but not 'ordinary' Catholics, who are seeking salvation rather than sanctification and perfection. However, this two-tier view is not that of the New Testament. Jesus is saying to each one of us, "Be perfect, therefore, as your heavenly Father is perfect" *(Matthew 5:48)*. Perhaps some members of the historic churches can at times learn something here from the new charismatic churches, who often seem to stress more than we do that Christianity is a call to give absolutely everything to God.

Having written the above I feel rather nervous lest some readers may go to extremes and do something God does not want them to do. For example, the fact that our bank account belongs to God does not normally mean that He wants us to give all our savings immediately to the Third World. I once heard of a lady who gave all her money to the poor and was a financial burden on her family and friends afterwards. It is very probable that some of my readers are giving more to charity than they should, and that God wants them to spend more money on healthy food, heating and an occasional holiday for themselves. It is also probable however that others of my readers are not giving away as much as God wants. The important thing is to try to give away as much as God wants, not the more the better. For some people in very difficult financial circumstances the right thing may be to give away nothing to charity, at least for the time being, although not a few people have found that as they gave, God provided.

Giving God one's time and energy will normally involve sacrifices at times, perhaps big ones. I have written earlier about the time given to prayer. What about work, hobbies, leisure, time given to family and friends? I met a man who had been pursuing a successful business career, who after prayer and reflection with his wife decided to give it up and go and work for a charity, where he remained until he retired. This involved having a considerably lower standard of living. I am sure God is calling some other Christians to make similar changes.

Then there is the university lecturer whom I know who used to enjoy playing chess for his university. Apparently, playing chess at that level involves spending quite a lot of time on chess. After prayer, he came to the conclusion that he was spending time on chess which he ought to give to his family and helping needy people, so he gave up playing chess for his university. Now, there is nothing wrong with playing chess, but the good can be the enemy of the better, and the better of the best So when we seek to spend our time and energy as God wills, when we seek to follow His perfect will, it is not enough to ask whether what I am doing is useful, bearing fruit, and helping others. We also have to ask is this the fruit God wants me to bear, or has He something different and better in mind. For example, a medical doctor may be doing a very good job helping the sick in England, but perhaps God would prefer him to go to a part of Africa where there is a much greater need for doctors.

Then there is the question of celibacy and marriage. Marriage is a good thing, indeed it is a sacrament. God is surely calling most people to marriage. However, Jesus is, I am convinced, calling some people to follow Him in the way of celibacy *(Matthew 19:12)* perhaps as a celibate priest or a religious. So the question people have to ask themselves is not whether marriage is a good thing, nor whether I would like to get married, but whether God is calling me to marriage. I know a woman who as she came out of the shop carrying her wedding dress was told by the Lord He wanted her to become a religious sister. After a difficult struggle she said Yes. And for some years now she has been living a very outstandingly fruitful life as a religious sister.

There is also the whole area of fasting, eating and drinking. Obviously we should seek to eat and drink all that God wants us to do and only that. Jesus not only gave us the example of fasting - "He fasted forty days and forty nights" *(Matthew 4:2)* - but He also assumed that we ourselves would fast He did not say if you fast, but "whenever you fast" *(Matthew 6:16)*. So some fasting from food should normally be a part of the Christian way of life, although of course there are people who for reasons of health should not fast from food, or should do so only very little.

In the matter of food and drink there is also the question of people eating and drinking unwisely when they should avoid doing so. Some people are ruining their health and shortening their lives by eating and drinking too much, or the wrong things, while, alas, millions of others in the world are more or less dying of starvation.

Again, I feel rather nervous that what I have written above may lead some Christians into excesses or fill them wrongly with feelings of guilt. St Anthony of Egypt gave away all his money to the poor, it is highly improbable that you are called to do the same. I know well a lady who fasted on a little weak tea and coffee for forty two days for the sake of a sick relative whose health improved most remarkably. She continued to cook for the family and drive the car around whilst fasting. Her husband, who is a medical consultant, checked her health regularly. It is most unlikely that God is calling you to fast for forty two days. If you are not already married and are a young person God is probably calling you to marriage, so do not start thinking that giving your life entirely to God will probably mean that He wants you to become a celibate priest or nun. Giving your life entirely to Jesus will also probably not mean giving up chess or tennis for good. Nor are most English doctors called to live in the Third World.

When Jesus is calling us to do something special he will normally in his time give us a particular attraction for it, and he will also give us the grace to see it through whatever the difficulties. In my own case, as a teenager, I had a number of girlfriends and never dreamed of the possibility of not getting married. However, after my conversion at the age of about 21, I felt strongly attracted to consecrated celibacy and was no longer interested in girlfriends. I was also no longer interested in the prospects of a successful business career. I remember Nicky Gumbel saying that earlier as a barrister the idea of being an Anglican priest would have appalled him, yet when the time came there was nothing he wanted more than ordination.

So if after prayer the idea of working with Aids patients, or becoming a missionary in Africa, or marrying that particular person, or joining a particular Christian community continues to fill you with dread or deep disquiet, then it is almost certain that God is not calling you in that direction, or at least not yet. We are all called to bear the Cross, to make sacrifices, even sometimes big sacrifices. But we are not called to carry every cross, only the one God chooses for us.

Jesus will give us the strength and grace and anointing we need for the cross He has chosen for us, but not for any other cross. It can be pride to think that because someone else fasts like that, spends nights in prayer like that, preaches like that, works late into the night like that, gives their money away like that, therefore I can or should be doing the same. We see in I Corinthians 12 that we are all different parts of the body. Disasters can happen if we seek to be a different part of the body than the one Jesus has chosen for us. Things will also go wrong if other people try to force me into a mould which is not God's will for me.

Jesus said to his Father in Gethsemanie, "My Father, if it is possible, let this cup pass from me; yet not what I want but what you want" *(Matthew 26:39)*. He also said that "I have come down from heaven, not to do my will, but the will of him who sent me" *(John 6:38)*.

Our Lady said, "Here am I, the servant of the Lord; let it be with me according to your word" *(Luke 1:38)*. We are all called to seek to follow the examples of Jesus and Mary and say Yes to God's perfect will for us. However, because we are sinners we tend to say, "Yes, but" rather than simply "Yes". "Yes, Lord, but do not touch my health, my bank account, my possessions, my career, my ministry, my reputation, this relationship, that hobby, my wife, my son, my daughter". Doubtless we do not normally say our "but" explicitly when we pray, but it can be there under the surface, sometimes very much so. **We need to remember that everything we give to Jesus is pure gain, and everything we withhold from him is loss.**

Our withholding from Jesus is not only sinful, it is also against our true self interest, indeed it is pathetic and stupid. If I have given everything to Jesus I am wonderfully secure, even if at the human level my position is very insecure. Insofar as I am outside the perfect will of Jesus through my own fault, I am insecure, however secure I may appear to be at the purely human level.

One very important event in our life to which it is especially important to try to say a complete "Yes" is our death. No one knows when we shall leave this life. Illnesses, accidents, violence, can and quite often do unexpectedly shorten people's lives. So we should be ready for death whenever it comes. It is good, I think, in advance to offer up our death to God and everything connected with it. And I also think it is or can be good to ask the Holy Spirit to show us for what intentions God wants us to offer up our death, indeed to offer up our life also. It might be, for example, for my family and for the peace of the world. In this way our death can be a moment of great fruitfulness, perhaps the most fruitful and meaningful moment of our life, as was the case with Jesus. (I believe very much in praying for healing and protection, but this will not, thank God, keep us alive on this earth for ever!). So if beforehand we have accepted and offered up our death, then if we are knocked over by a car or are hit by a heart attack, it has already been accepted and given to God.

I must admit that I sometimes feel fearful at the thought of what Jesus may call me to do or suffer - I am temperamentally a rather fearful person. However, saying "Yes" is not only the right thing to do, it is also the safest. Jesus is still saying, "Follow me". If by the grace of God I do that, then there is nothing to fear. He has seen me through the trials and sufferings of the past, and he will, I trust, continue to do so until one day I am with Him in the glorious heavenly banquet.

Alleluia, Alleluia, Alleluia!

Chapter Five
Listening to God

Of the five areas of prayer which I mentioned earlier, listening to God is normally by a long way the one which is most neglected. Prayer is meant to be a dialogue with God, but so often prayer is just a monologue or nearly so, and poor God can hardly get a word in edgeways! When the Lord called Samuel, he replied: "Speak, for your servant is listening" *(I Samuel 3:10)*. So often we simply say, "Listen, Lord your servant is speaking".

"Be still, and know that I am God" *(Psalm 46:10)*. In our prayer life we should deliberately set enough time aside to be still, to listen to God. I confess that I quite often neglect this side of prayer, but when I manage to do it, it is so often fruitful.

We should listen to God about our agenda, but also about His. We might be asking God to show us whether we should read a particular book, visit a person in need, volunteer for a task, resign from our job - and it is right that we should try to listen to God on such things. However, God may have something more important to say to us: "Forgive and love that person", "fast more", "Be financially more generous", "Get up earlier to pray", "Stop flirting with that person". I have found that when I have asked God to speak His word to me, quite often what came to me was not something I particularly wanted to hear! Indeed, sometimes over quite a period God has gone on saying something which I was finding difficult. That made me think all the more that it almost

31

certainly did come from God.

Before I go any further, I must reassure readers that I do not think that I have an infallible hot line to God! Often I pray about a problem and seem to get no reply from God. At other times I am doubting whether what I seem to be hearing really is from God - perhaps it is simply my wishful thinking. And even if I feel confident that something has come from God, I have to remember that I can be mistaken. Once I felt strongly that God was saying to me that a seriously ill elderly person with whom we were praying for healing was going to die soon. Now, several years later, that person is still running around and living a fruitful life!

How does God guide us, speak to us? In the Bible there are of course many examples of God speaking very directly to people. For example, there is the call of Abram in Genesis 12, and Moses at the burning bush *(Exodus 3)*. Indeed, the Lord spoke frequently to the Old Testament patriarchs and prophets.

In the New Testament the angel Gabriel foretells the births of St John the Baptist and Jesus *(Luke 2)*, St Joseph is told in dreams to accept Mary as his wife *(Matthew 1)*, to flee to Egypt and to return from Egypt *(Matthew 2)*. Indeed, in the New Testament events are continually guided by the Holy Spirit, sometimes dramatically so. One has only to think of the conversion *(Acts 9)* and life of St Paul, in which there are quite a number of direct divine interventions, for example, St Paul and St Barnabas sent out on a mission *(Acts 13)*, the vision calling them to Macedonia *(Acts 16)*, and the message of the angel during the storm at sea *(Acts 27)*.

There is also in the New Testament the key event for

the future of Christianity of the acceptance of pagans as Christians, linked with revelations to Cornelius and St Peter *(Acts 10)*. Then there is St Peter's liberation from prison *(Acts 12)*. In the New Testament God so often intervenes and guides clearly.

In the lives of the Saints we also frequently see examples of direct and explicit guidance, as when St Anthony of Egypt was told to sell all his property and give the money to the poor, or when St Bernadette of Lourdes was given messages for the parish priest. This sort of guidance is not only something of the past. Sr Breige McKenna was praying in the chapel alone one day when she heard an audible voice saying that she had a gift of healing. She turned round to see who had spoken and was surprised to see no one there. Then more than one person came up to her and said that they thought God was saying that she had a gift of healing. She resisted the vocation to the healing ministry for quite a time, but eventually gave in. Since then she has travelled in many countries of the world exercising a very fruitful and powerful healing and evangelistic ministry.

One can also mention the prophetic word spoken to Nicky Gumbel of Holy Trinity, Brompton and Alpha by John Wimber, saying that God was giving Nicky a special gift as an evangelist, a word which has been wonderfully confirmed by events.

However, it needs to be said very clearly that divine guidance is not normally something dramatic involving things like special messages or visions. Indeed, God usually speaks to us and guides us in much more ordinary ways. Perhaps we are wondering which of two courses of action we should take, and after prayer we may simply and peacefully feel that one is right and the other not. Sometimes God's guidance comes to us through the decisions of others in authority, or through external circumstances. A parent may be wondering whether God wants them to take a holiday abroad, and then one of the children becomes seriously ill and there is no question of taking such a holiday. God also guides us very often through the right use of that wonderful faculty, the gift of reason. Someone may be wondering whether to buy a house, but a more careful consideration of all the financial factors involved may clearly show that buying the house is not possible,

Obviously, decisions of greater importance require more careful discernment. One should not spend too long on deciding whether to go shopping this afternoon or reply to letters. However, if it is a question of deciding whether to study medicine or classics at the university, of entering a seminary, of marrying someone, of emigrating to America, of volunteering for missionary work in Africa, of buying a house, then clearly much more time and attention normally needs to be given to discernment. In important matters we should normally when possible consult other suitable people and also get others to pray about the decision. In that way we are less likely to be deceived by our own imagination, muddle-headedness, prejudices, or the devil. In important decisions we should normally expect to get confirmations from other suitable people.

I remember when some years ago a particular group of Christians were planning to smuggle Bibles into Russia by car. They had to choose which of many routes to take, and they prayed much about this, for if things went wrong they would not only lose the Bibles, but it could be very dangerous for the Russians who received the Bibles - they could end up in Siberia. So having decided on a particular route they said that they would not go unless they received five independent confirmations as to the rightness of the route. They received their confirmations, and all went well with the smuggling operation.

If we are seeking the guidance of the Holy Spirit on a particular question, we should place the matter in God's hands, be willing to obey whatever guidance may be given - sometimes easier said than done - and try to listen to God, noting any signs which may come along. It can also be good to ask God to close the doors He wishes to close and open those He wishes to open. One good friend of mine had been asked by this wife to attend an Alpha course with her at Holy Trinity Brompton. He replied, "Certainly not". A day or so later a friend with whom he was playing tennis suggested he might like to attend an Alpha course, and then very soon after another person made the same suggestion. He realised that God might be saying something to him through these 'coincidences', so he decided to go to Alpha with his wife and it profoundly changed his life. He now runs Alpha courses very effectively for others.

I personally tend quite often to get a sort of interior word which comes into my mind. It is frequently "Yes" or "No" to a question I have asked God. It might also be for example, "now", or "wait", or "soon", or "beware", or "speak to him", or "enough", or buy it", or "stop", or "courage". Indeed such words may come into my mind when I am not specially listening. People who are more gifted than myself in this field - and there are many of them - often receive much more developed words of knowledge, such as "there is someone here who God is wanting to heal of heart sickness, and this person's work is involved with legal documents". (This was an actual case in our prayer group which was confirmed by the healing which took place on a man who worked with legal documents). Or, it could be, "there is someone here who had an accident when they were ten, and God wants to heal their leg". Needless to say, it is normally very important that only people whose gifts have been tested should be allowed to give out publicly such words of knowledge, otherwise harm can be done. And it is always necessary to remember that such words of knowledge are never infallible - no one is so gifted that they could never be mistaken.

St Ignatius of Loyola, who is regarded as a special authority on the subject of discernment, stressed in discernment the importance of deep peace. If someone is wondering whether or not God wants them to follow a certain course of action, they should pray seriously about it and then see if they experience a deep inner peace when they reflect on that course of action.   This deep inner peace can be seen as God's confirmation. In his famous Spiritual Exercises *(54)* St Ignatius wrote: "I will find that I speak or listen as God's Spirit moves me".

When having a counselling or healing session with someone I normally suggest that after we have prayed and talked we should listen to God in silence for a time. Quite often a word then comes into my mind. Once, at a time when I was Prior of our community, I was seeing a guest who wanted to stay in the monastery for quite a long time. I got the word "beware". I could not think what I had to beware of. This guest had a rather refined accent and said that he had received a first class honours degree in Oxford - later I discovered that the last point was true. He also said that he had a cancer operation, which was also true. However, because of the word "beware" I was being more vigilant than I would otherwise have been, and I discovered that some of the things he was saying about his cancer treatment clearly were not true. We had to ask him to leave. Soon after he was back in prison once more, this time for stealing works of art from an Oxford College. Some years later I read in a newspaper that he had just been given a prison sentence of over twenty years. Say a prayer for him. I burned my fingers a little with this man, but I would probably have done so much more without the warning "beware".

Normally I pray before buying things like clothes and books, and on the whole over the years this seems to have been truly fruitful. I once went off to London to buy a pair of shoes. I went into Selfridges, found a very suitable pair, except that they were, I thought, too expensive for a monk. So I decided to look elsewhere. I passed a shop, thought from the contents of the shop window that it did not look promising, and was passing on to the next shop, when I seemed to get a clear inner nudge to go back to the one I had rejected. I went in and saw that manager, who tried to sell me some shoes which were too expensive and uncomfortable. Then out of the corner of my eye I noticed some solid, broad shoes which looked the right sort of thing for me. The manager said they were just casual shoes from Poland, and in disgust left me to an assistant. The shoes were just what I wanted and were incredibly cheap. So I bought two pairs, and a third pair a week later. These shoes lasted me for years. Just chance? I do not think so.

However, shopping expeditions do not always end as expected. My warm heavy coat needed mending and both friends and a dry cleaner said it was not mendable. So I thought I must go and buy a new heavy coat - and I thought that I had prayed sufficiently about it. I arrived at the top of the underground escalators near the shop, I said a prayer to the Lord, "You do want me to buy that warm coat, don't you?" And I got a resounding inner "No", so I returned to the bottom of the escalator and prayed again. The answer was still "No", so I returned back to the monastery without the coat. A short time afterwards I tried another dry cleaning shop, and they happily mended the coat without too much difficulty.

Some people might object that in a world where there is so much suffering and so many needy people, a priest should have more important things to do than seek God's guidance about buying shoes or coats. However, I think God has a loving plan for each one of us, and that this plan includes details, even such things as parking meters. Jesus said, "Are not two sparrows sold for a penny? Yet not one of them will fall to the ground apart from your Father. And even the hairs of your head are numbered". (Most obviously so in my case at the age of 78!). "So do not be afraid, you are of more value than many sparrows" *(Matthew 10:29)*. So I think that God's loving Providence covers the small things as well as the big. When we experience His loving care in small things that can increase our trust in Him for the big ones, which may often seem hopeless or very difficult at the human level.

However, a warning needs to be given here. Some people can go over the top about 'guidance from the Holy Spirit'. Some years ago a priest asked me to see a man whom he was worried about. The man had previously had a kind of conversion experience and was convinced that the Holy Spirit was guiding him in almost every detail of his life. It was soon clear to us that he was imagining lots of things, including details about how and where he was to sit and when and what he was to eat. We suggested that he see a doctor, but he would not. We told him clearly that we were convinced that he was suffering from delusions, but he would not or could not listen to us. When he left us he agreed to see a sister involved in counselling. I hope that she succeeded better than we did! There are times when some people need to be discouraged from too much listening to the Holy Spirit.

We all need at times to seek confirmation from others, to be willing to be checked out by one or more other suitable people, perhaps a doctor, a confessor, or a spiritual friend. If we are not wise and humble enough to accept the judgement of other suitable people when necessary, then our own fantasies and the devil can play havoc with our lives.

Some people may think that trying to listen to God is too hazardous because of the danger of mistakes and of going over the top. Is it not better just to rely on reason and Christian common sense? Definitely not, at least in general. The saints are, I think, the right example for us to try to follow in this matter. Many of the saints were led in ways more or less similar to St Paul in the New Testament. Let us consider, for example, the lives of St Teresa of Avila, the Cure d'Ars, and Padre Pio. How much less fruitful they would have been if they had not received remarkable divine guidance. Think of Padre Pio. Because of his supernatural words of knowledge (revelations) Padre Pio was able to greatly help and enlighten large numbers of people in a relatively short time. Not that we should think that we are another Padre Pio or St Teresa of Avila - that indeed would be spiritual pride and dangerous. But inspired and encouraged by their example we can seek to move in their direction.

As for myself, being something of a lame duck, would I not be better in giving up my quest for divine guidance and leaving that to holy people? No! Despite the mistakes I make, I am sure that my life would be less fruitful for Jesus if I stopped trying to listen to Him. Indeed, as calls on time and energy have multiplied, I am finding it more and more desirable and necessary to try to listen increasingly to him. Certainly I need at times to check the guidance I think I am receiving with other suitable people, including my monastic superior, the leaders of our prayer group, and my doctor. However, if there are dangers in trying to listen to the Lord, there are far bigger ones in not doing so.

The practical circumstances in which we find ourselves in life are frequently very complex. So many factors concerning the present and the future are uncertain. For example, one's health and the health of others, the uncertainty of how other people are going to react to situations, the economic and political climate in our country and the world. So however intelligent we are, however learned, very often our reason cannot take us far in foreseeing what is going to happen, and in knowing what is the best course of action. That is why, alas, increasing numbers of people are turning to fortune tellers and clairvoyants, which can be very dangerous. Jesus however, knows the future and all its circumstances. His plan for us takes into account our future circumstances. So if we can learn to listen to Him, that can protect us from going down blind alleys and making many mistakes.

Doubtless there will be people who will criticise me for being personal in this chapter, as elsewhere in this book. Writers on prayer, it will be said, do not usually say so much about their own life of prayer. However, I think that by being personal this book is likely to help some readers more. I myself have benefited from the testimony tradition in the Charismatic Renewal and elsewhere. Of course the testimony aspect can be overdone. Whether or not I have overdone it readers will have to decide for themselves. What I can say, however, is very much in line with the words of Our Lord to St Paul: "My grace is sufficient for you, for My power is made perfect in weakness" *(2 Corinthians 12:9)*.

Listening To God Through Holy Scripture

In this book on prayer obviously something needs to be written about the prayerful reading of the Bible, and the chapter on listening to God seems to be the best place for that, since the Holy Spirit often speaks to us through

Holy Scripture. This is in part an embarrassing subject for me, since I am only too aware that I do not know the Bible as well as I should and I do not spend enough time reading it, given the opportunities I have long had.

Of course as a priest and a monk I hear much of the Bible read in the liturgy. However, for me the biblical readings in the liturgy do not usually sink in as much as when I am reading the Bible on my own and am able to take my time over it, perhaps reading a particular passage several times. Indeed to be truthful, by the end of Mass I have very often forgotten what was the first reading.

I try to spend time daily on spiritual reading (lectio divina) of the Bible, which is something different from an academic study of the Bible, which study also has a real value and place, but that is outside the scope of this book. Spiritual reading of the Bible is very much part of the monastic Benedictine tradition and St Benedict in his Rule sets aside time daily for it. Alas, sometimes the pressures of other things and my own lack of discipline cause me to drop my daily Bible reading. When this happens too often I feel that my spiritual life suffers. There is, I think, normally no substitute for a prayerful reading of the Bible and letting God speak to us and free us through His Word - at least that is my experience.

Before reading we should surely say a prayer to the Holy Spirit and ask Him to illuminate our minds and touch our hearts, ask Him to feed us and speak to us through God's Word. We might, for example, read a passage of the New Testament on forgiveness and this may bring to mind someone we have not fully forgiven. Or we might be reading a passage about trusting God, and this may help us to trust God more in matters of health or material needs. Or we might be going through a very difficult time of suffering, and reading Jesus' words about denying oneself and taking up one's cross daily *(Luke 9:23)* might give us new strength.

How should we set about reading the Bible? As the Holy Spirit leads us, the Spirit will guide different people in different ways. For many years now my regular Bible reading has normally been going through the New Testament from Matthew to Revelation and then starting again. Sometimes however I feel led to read a particular passage or book. And periodically (too rarely) I read through the Old Testament from beginning to end. However the Holy Spirit may lead you in a very different way. Some may like to concentrate more on the daily readings of the Mass or the Divine Office. Others will find it helpful to follow the order of one or other of the booklets which give daily readings with a commentary which follows the daily Mass reading, such as Bible Alive *(Graphic House, 124 City Road, Stoke on Trent ST4 2PH)* and Every Day with Jesus, *(Scripture Union, Selwyn Hughes, CAR Waverley Abbey House, Waverley Lane, Farnham, Surrey GU9 8EP)*. Obviously, Bibles with notes and Bible commentaries can also be very helpful.

It can also, I think, be very helpful for our own prayer life, indeed for our Christian life as a whole, to know by heart parts of the Bible. Then at the right moment the Holy Spirit can bring to mind the appropriate text, perhaps a passage for our own needs, perhaps a passage to help us when we are ministering to others. Alas, I personally have a poor literary memory, so I just have to try to manage as best I can - and try not to be envious of those who know the Bible much better than I do!

Two other things can help us to know the Bible. The first is to mark passages, perhaps in different colours. This certainly helps me to find passages I am looking for. The second is the practice of normally reading the same translation of the Bible. I think it can be good sometimes to read a text in another translation, but if we normally stick to the same translation that will enable us to remember texts better. It is good to ask the Holy Spirit to lead us in our choice of translation. Finally, many Christians find it helpful to have written Bible texts on their walls or elsewhere. I have three beautiful tiles with "Be still and know that I am God" *(Psalm 45)*, "Be filled with the Holy Spirit" *(Ephesians 5:18)*, and "Alleluia". These tiles certainly help my life of prayer at times as I look upon them on the wall in my room.

At the end of this section I am concerned lest some readers may feel that their cultural limitations and busy lives will mean that they will always be very much second class Christians when it comes to being fed by the Word of God through the Bible. A mother with young children, a sick husband, and a job may well feel that my recommendations to read the Bible daily and learn texts by heart is utopian for someone like her. To which I reply, "Do what you can and be at peace. God does not expect the impossible."

However, there is another important point which is relevant here. The blessings we receive from a prayerful reading of the Bible are not in proportion to the amount we read or to our knowledge of the Bible. Indeed the learned Biblical professor who may sometimes have largely forgotten that the Bible is the Word of God, may in fact receive less spiritual nourishment from the Bible than the busy housewife who cannot remember whether the gospel of Luke comes after or before John's gospel. It can be good to learn Hebrew and Greek and read commentaries - thank God for sound learning - but the prayerfulness and faith with which we read or listen to God's Word in the Bible are the key factors when it comes to being spiritually nourished and blessed through the Bible.

A last point. Given the importance of reading God's Word in the Bible, I am frequently surprised to find how some Christians who think nothing about spending money on an expensive meal in a restaurant or on a distant foreign holiday seem to think that they cannot afford to buy a decent Bible or a bible commentary. Priorities? Perhaps some readers of this chapter should go out and treat themselves to a new and expensive Bible! And having bought this new Bible, let them put it in a place of honour in their homes and not just leave it to gather dust or lie at the bottom of a pile of books. I think many Catholics could often learn from our evangelical brothers and sisters when it comes to respect for and knowledge of God's Word in the Bible.

Chapter Six
Intercession I

"And he said to them, 'Suppose one of you has a friend, and you go to him at midnight and say to him, Friend, lend me three loaves of bread; for a friend of mine has arrived, and I have nothing to set before him.' And he answers from within, 'Do not bother me; the door has already been locked, and my children are with me in bed; I cannot get up and give you anything.' I tell you, even though he will not get up and give him anything because he is his friend, at least because of his persistence he will get up and give him whatever he needs. So I say to you. Ask, and it will be given you, search, and you will find; knock and the door will be opened for you. For everyone who asks receives, and everyone who searches finds, and for everyone who knocks the door will be opened. Is there anyone among you who, if your child asks for a fish, will give a snake instead of a fish? Or if the child asks for an egg, will you give a scorpion? If you then, who are evil, know how to give good gifts to your children, how much more will the heavenly Father give the Holy Spirit to those who ask him!" *(Luke 11:5-13).*

Last Monday evening at our prayer meeting of about one hundred people, we prayed over a sincere and committed Catholic who at 2pm that afternoon was in a Crown Court as the accused person at the start of a case before a judge and jury. The defending barrister expected the case to last until Friday. The person in question had doubtless been naive and unwise, but was not a criminal. There was a distinct possibility of the case ending with a prison sentence, which is what the police were expecting. So we stormed heaven.

On Tuesday morning, to the great amazement of everyone, including the defending barrister, the judge dismissed the whole case with vigour. The barrister, a lapsed Catholic, said to the defendant: "You have definitely got Someone looking after you". I am not claiming that there would not have been the same result if there had been no prayer. Even less am I saying that prayer will always produce results like that. However, I do think that things like that are far more likely to happen when there has been serious prayer - and an increasing number of Christians in our times seem to be finding that to be true from their own experience.

(I remember another somewhat similar legal case some years ago now, when much prayer was followed by a result which the defending solicitor and barrister said was impossible).

Of course many of us have prayed seriously, sometimes over a long period, for intentions which have not been answered as we first hoped. Perhaps we prayed for someone's cancer to be healed, and they died. Perhaps we prayed for a marriage to stick together and the spouses separated. Perhaps we prayed for someone to come back to the Church and they died without doing so. Perhaps we prayed for someone to find employment, and they remained unemployed. Perhaps we prayed for an alcoholic to stop drinking, and he died because of drink.

Does that mean that we were mistaken in praying as

we did? Maybe in some cases, yes. Maybe sometimes if we had listened to God more clearly, we would have prayed otherwise.   Perhaps in other cases if there had been more prayer and fasting, the results would have been different. But very often we were right to pray as we did, and God simply did not choose to answer our prayers as we first hoped. However, if we have prayed authentically, God will have blessed the people or situation in one way or another through our prayers.

Let us take a hypothetical situation. Let us suppose that there is a real danger of nuclear war breaking out between England and France next week. Surely we should all pray and storm heaven that the war does not happen, that the politicians and military men are led by the Holy Spirit in the direction of peace and justice. If the war did break out that does not mean that we were mistaken in praying for peace. Nor does it mean that God did not hear our prayers. Perhaps because we and others prayed only five bombs were dropped instead of ten.

Jesus told us to pray - "Ask and it will be given to you, search and you will find; knock and the door will be opened for you" *(Luke 11:9)* - and when we pray authentically, which by the grace of God we always can do, then our prayers will be heard and situations and people will be blessed in one way or another, even if only in a very small way.

Obviously, all our intercessions must be subject to "Thy will be done on earth as it is in heaven" *(Matthew 6:10)*. However, I am worried when some Christians seem to suggest that is the only request we ever need to make. When Jesus taught us to pray the Our Father, He did not stop with "Thy will be done", He went on with the other requests, including "Give us this day our daily bread" and "deliver us from the evil one".

I think we can learn here from the example of many of the outstanding saints in all our churches. They did not, do not, only pray "Thy will be done", they also frequently storm heaven for such things as the conversion of a particular individual, the healing of a sick person, the money for building a church or an orphanage, and for God's protection and blessing on a difficult journey. Now, these prayers will not always have been answered as they first hoped, but quite often they will have been.

One meets beautiful Christians in all our churches who fairly frequently experience answers to prayer. Nicky Gumble of Holy Trinity, Brompton and the Alpha course has told us that he writes down in a note-book his petitions, and goes through ticking them off if and when they are answered. He is not the only person to do that or something similar.

Indeed, I think it should be normal that Christians experience answers to prayers, and not so infrequently, and in my opinion something is missing in a Christian's life when someone says they do not experience these answers. It is often in the little things that we most frequently experience answers. Somebody prays for a headache to go, and it goes quickly. Many Christians pray for parking meters, and they assure us, rightly I think, that it so often seems to make a difference. As I said in the last chapter, when I pray before buying clothes I often seem to get just the right thing. I also find that when I have to prepare a homily or talk and my head is empty of ideas (frequently the case), it is after prayer that the ideas and the inspirations come, sometimes rather at the last moment.

William Temple, the great Archbishop of Canterbury, replied to those who said that what he believed were answers to prayer were just coincidences: "All I know is that when I pray these 'coincidences' happen, and when I stop praying they do not".

Some people may object that praying for parking meters or for an ordinary headache to be healed rather trivialises prayer, when there are so many more important intentions to pray for, like peace in the world or someone dying of cancer. For me, it is not a question of one or the other - we should pray for the small things and pray for the big ones. Receiving an answer to prayer in a small matter can increase our faith and perseverance for the important intentions. If God in His loving care for me, for us, is even interested in finding us a parking meter - by the way I do not drive - then He is certainly looking after the bigger problems, such as a forthcoming major operation, or a son who is a drug addict, or peace and justice in connection with Ireland. It is normal in life that sooner or later we all have to face bigger problems which call for ongoing prayer, perhaps for many years or until the end of our life. The small answers can encourage us to persevere with the long haul and the difficult mountains.

I am saddened when I meet Christians, even some serious and dedicated Christians, whose confidence in the power of prayer is or seems to be so limited. A priest who is highly trained in psychotherapy told me that he did not believe in praying for physical healing, for himself or for others. Many Christians would not it seems, believe in praying for protection on a difficult journey, or a job, or for the conversion of a non-Christian, or that God would protect their homes from burglars. I think that many Christians have in varying degrees been largely taken over by the prevailing secularist intellectual climate around us. Science and psychology seem often to have replaced Christian faith as their main point of reference.

So they would say that praying for a safe journey in a car, for oneself or others, is really rather superstitious, since God does not intervene directly in such matters in answer to our prayers. Prayer, some others would think, is for spiritual matters, and therefore we should not bother God about our physical and material needs. I remember one business man, who would not miss Sunday Mass and who prayed daily, telling me that he never prayed for God's blessing on his business, which took up so much of his time and energy. He thought that his business life was not a suitable subject for prayer.

If, however, we have really given our lives to God, to Jesus, despite our weakness and sinfulness, then He is certainly really concerned with every aspect of our lives, including our health, or finances, our relationships, our sex life, our hobbies. So we can and should pray about these things, because they all have a part to play in the building up of God's Kingdom. If there is anything I am doing which I should not ask for God's blessing on, then I should not be doing it. It would, indeed, for example, be inappropriate to ask for God's blessing on my evening's occupation if I am going out to mug people! Insofar as I have really given my life to God, to

Jesus, then my interests are His interests, and I should ask for God's blessing on them.

Needless to say, science and psychology are in themselves good and we should make a right use of them in building up God's Kingdom. Where things go wrong is when they wholly or in part replace the vision of Christian faith, and I think this happens fairly often.

God, of course, can have very good reasons for not answering our prayers, as we first hoped. It may, for example, be highly desirable for the safety of everyone concerned that someone does not pass their driving test! It may also be a very good thing if someone does not succeed in an exam if they are in fact setting out on studies which are not the right one's for them. It may be a blessing when God does not answer a prayer for great material success, if in fact the success would spiritually corrupt the person in question. Billy Graham's wife has said that if God had answered her prayers as she first hoped, she would more than once have married the wrong man - the Grahams have an exceptionally happy marriage.

This reminds us of the importance of always praying subject to God's perfect will. It also reminds us of the desirability of trying to listen to God before praying, as explained in the last chapter. Although God can sort out our mistaken prayers when there is sincerity, yet it is obviously better to pray explicitly as far as we can in line with His perfect will.

For whom and for what should we intercede? How should we intercede? The short answer is, as the Holy

Spirit leads us. And, to repeat, the Holy Spirit will lead no two people in exactly the same way, nor shall we be led in exactly the same way this year as last year, for our life of prayer should not be static but growing. So what I am writing now are not fixed rules to be rigidly followed, but guidelines or hints to be followed insofar as they are found to be helpful.

The Holy Spirit will I think, normally lead us to intercede right along a line, so to speak, with ourselves at one end of the line and the whole Church and world at the other, with numerous intentions for prayer in between. To concentrate too much on myself would be selfish, to pray too little for myself would be a lack of the right kind of self-love - "love your neighbour as yourself" *(Matthew22: 39)* not, "love your neighbour and not yourself". In any case, insofar as I myself am not in right order, I cannot help others.

We should normally surely pray daily by name for the close members of our family, concentrating especially for those whose needs are greater, for example at a special time of trial, danger or temptation, a serious operation, a particular opportunity or an important decision. Something is wrong if we are neglecting to pray for our family.

Then we should also pray for our friends, our 'enemies' (most important), our neighbours, those we work with. Surely there is something missing if Christians never pray for the people they live next to, work with, mix with. Then we should also pray, I would think, for the people we worship with at church or in the prayer group and for the clergy. Yes, please pray for your clergy. If you think they are very wonderful, pray that God may sustain them and keep them humble, and if you regard them as 'useless', as a woman said to me of a priest this week, pray that God may make them less 'useless', indeed really fruitful!

Then there are the people we meet in our daily life: the drunken man we see in the road, the homeless person in the doorway, the over-exhausted mother shouting at her child, the prostitute we pass in the street, the blind man with his white stick, the sick woman suffering greatly in the hospital ward, the person going by in the ambulance, the extravagant worshipper of mammon, the bullying boss, the physically or mentally handicapped child. We may not be in a position to give practical help, but we can always send up a short prayer - and perhaps continue to pray later.

I try to say a prayer for the people with whom I am sharing an underground carriage. It is usually a very short prayer. Often I forget. And I have no illusions that my prayer has converted half a dozen people and healed the blind! - though we can never put limits to God's goodness. If one person greets their spouse on returning home with a smile instead of a scowl, then my prayer was worthwhile.

The media can feed our intercession wonderfully. One past member of our prayer group who has now left this district called her daily newspaper her "prayer book". She used to go through the various items which she felt called for prayer. The whole process would sometimes take her three hours - she lived on her own. Remembering her example, when I read a newspaper I start, if I have not forgotten, by making a large sign of the Cross over the front page, and then I make a sign of the cross or say a short prayer or both over items which seem to call especially for it - the war in Yugoslavia, the people hit by the earthquake in Columbia, the convicted murderer, the raped girl, the debate in parliament on aid to the Third World or abortion.

In a way it is sub-Christian to watch starving or suffering people on TV or learning about them through other forms of the media without saying a prayer for them and the situation. However, we cannot always rise to a fully Christian response, being surrounded as we are by so many needs and evils - not to mention our own lack of love.

Many Christians, and I am one of them, find it helpful to have an intercession list. Some people pray for or concentrate on different intentions on difference days of the week, for example, for peace on Mondays, for evangelisation on Tuesdays. I personally do not do that. My daily lists includes numerous individual names, but also some collective groups or intentions like our prayer group, our parish, peace and justice in the world, and the outpouring of the Holy Spirit over the world. It takes me normally about fifteen minutes to go through my list, depending on how distracted or busy I am. If I have flu or am very fully caught up with some apostolic work, I may drop the list altogether for a few days, apart from saying a brief collective prayer for all those on the list. However, I feel something is missing if I unnecessarily neglect the list, and I am happy to get back to it again. We must not be a slave to things like lists, but some of us find that they are a very real help to prayer. I normally read through the list fairly quickly but taking longer, sometimes much longer, when there is a special need or when feeling inspired to do so. Personally I use the gift of tongues much when going through my list, but I will write more about that gift later.

St Thérèse of Lisieux, if I remember rightly, used at one time to use prayer lists for her intercession, but later felt called to give up the lists and just intercede as the Holy Spirit led her. Fine. But many of us who have not arrived at her openness to the Holy Spirit will find lists helpful, especially if our memory for names is not what it was! However, her example can remind all of us that we must not be bound by lists and devotions, and that all must be led by the Holy Spirit.

The Holy Spirit inspires different people in different ways when it comes to intercession. I know one elderly man living in a London suburb who tries to pray for the people whom he meets walking in the opposite direction on the pavement - that would hardly be possible in a busy city centre. A contemplative nun whose convent is not very far from an international airport prays for the people in the planes she hears above. A motorist I know lifts up in prayer the people in the surrounding cars when he is caught up in a traffic jam. A member of our prayer group when driving in a built up area from time-to-time asks God to bless the people who live in the homes on both sides of the road. A friend of mine living in one of a block of flats for the elderly, daily prays down the list of the people living in the flats - it takes about 15 minutes. A surgeon I know prays "In the name of the Father, Son, and the Holy Spirit" as she cuts through the skin. (Incidentally, once when she was assisting another surgeon in an operation things went very wrong and it looked as through the patient would die quickly from loss of blood. My friend prayed desperately for the bleeding to stop and it did, to the great surprise and relief of the main surgeon).

I mention these examples not so that others should copy them, but so that each one of us may find what is right for us in the way of intercession. I am aware, of course, that a busy mother of young children or an overworked hospital doctor probably have more than enough on their minds without trying to pray for people in aeroplanes above. However, ask the Holy Spirit to show you if He wants to influence you in any way through these examples.

In church congregations there is normally some way of encouraging prayer for the sick and other intentions. We have here an intercession book in the entrance hall of our church, where people can write in the names of sick people and of the recently dead. In every Mass, as elsewhere, there are the bidding prayers, and we read out the names of sick people and the departed. In our prayer group we have an intercession book where people can write in their intentions, and they are encouraged also to put their thank you's for answers to prayer at the back of the book. At our monthly Day of Renewal in Euston two baskets are provided for people to put in their written intentions, and the baskets are placed on the altar during the Mass. In many churches and prayer groups there are prayer vigils for special intentions, (I personally am better on the 8.30-10.30 p.m. vigils than those which go on until 6.00 a.m!).

Chapter Seven
Intercession II

In the Catholic tradition religious communities, especially contemplative communities, have a special intercessory role, and these communities often receive many requests for prayer. One Carmelite nun from the convent in Ware explained to me how they put up requests for prayer on a notice board outside the chapel so that the sisters can, so to speak, carry the intentions with them for other sisters to read, and they share requests for intercessions with each other spontaneously during the community recreation. They, of course, pray for the various crises in the world reported in the media.

Then of course Christians sometimes go on a pilgrimage to some special place like Jerusalem or Lourdes largely to pray for a particular intention such as a sick person, or a marriage situation, or for peace and justice in say Northern Ireland. In recent years there have been the rapidly expanding 'Marches for Jesus' in many countries in the world, which are not only a powerful witness, but which include much intercession.

Groups of Christians, mainly, I think, on the Evangelical-Pentecostal side, are going out to pray before places of what may be termed 'strategic importance'. Recently a small group of us from our prayer group did a 'pray-around' in part of central London. I was celebrating the 11.00 a.m. parish weekday Mass. After the Mass we set out down the road towards our underground station ten minutes walk away. We prayed for the people living in the houses on either side, for the shops and the pub. We prayed for the staff in the station and for the underground system as a whole. We prayed for the people in our underground carriages. We got out at Leicester Square and prayed briefly in the French church there for the clergy and congregation and all that happened there. We had a brief meal, praying for the people in the restaurant. We walk around Soho for a short time, praying for an area which in some places has not got a good reputation. (I had wanted to pray in front of an 'immoral house', as the Soho prayer group used to do, but the women in our group guided us towards more salubrious areas!) We also went into a Christian bookshop in Soho and prayed for their mission to the Chinese and for the lady who ran the shop.

We prayed in several churches, including the Methodist Central Hall, Westminster Abbey and Westminster Cathedral. We prayed before Downing Street for Tony Blair and his family, for the Cabinet and for all that happened in Downing Street. We prayed for the centres of the Civil Service, for police in New Scotland Yard and for the police everywhere, for a bank and the whole banking community, and for Premier Christian Radio, which is doing so much for God's Kingdom. We prayed for people in cars, for the homeless and for the alcoholics. We also thanked God for beautiful flowers in St James' Park. Everywhere we prayed we felt it important to mix our intercessions with much praise and thanksgiving.

Our whole outing took about six and a half hours. It was a joyful if tiring time, and we felt it was very worthwhile. From the point of view of building up

God's Kingdom I think it was truly fruitful, considerably more fruitful than most six and a half hour periods during my day. Doubtless our prayer group will do more such outings. Perhaps one way in which it will prove to have been helpful will be in encouraging us to do more interceding as we normally travel around, and where I at any rate normally miss so many opportunities.

One intercession movement which is spreading rapidly is 'Mothers Prayers'. Christian mothers in smaller or bigger numbers meet together regularly to pray for their children. It may be only two or three mothers in the home of one of them, it may be quite a large group. The incredibly quick growth of this movement in different countries shows how it is answering a very special need. It obviously helps and encourages Christian mothers to get together to pray for their children. The mothers have much to be concerned about with regard to the environment in which their children are growing up, for example, television, sexual promiscuity, drugs, bullying in schools, violence, scientific secularism. *(address: 'Mothers Prayers' P.O. Box 822, Gravesend, Kent DA13 9ZZ - Tel 01474 834084).*

'Prayer Diaries' are fairly common. I have before me a Catholic prayer diary produced by the Youth Mission Team of the Catholic diocese of Hexham and Newcastle. It covers three months, and every day it mentions a school or parish where they are ministering, or the names of a member of their team, or something connected with their ministry. In this way their ministry is assured of more prayer backing, which they rightly regard as of fundamental importance.

Prayer chains or links can be a special help when

there is an urgent need of prayer. If there is a sudden crisis such as an accident or an unexpected operation in hospital, in our prayer group we can phone a particular member and she sets in motion the prayer chain so that within half an hour, twenty or more people are praying for the particular intention.

In the leadership team of the prayer group we are committed to pray for each other by name every day. This is a source of very helpful support and unity. Relationships are different when people are praying for each other by name every day. In a monastery also the mutual prayer for each other is clearly very important.

The telephone can be very useful when it comes to prayer, not only to let people know of needs, but also to pray aloud for healing and other intentions over the phone. I personally spend quite a bit of time praying for people in this way, for healing and other intentions. If someone asks me to pray for this or that coming event, I often just pray on the spot - perhaps on the telephone. Otherwise, I find myself promising to pray for something and forgetting to do so. More important future intentions I put in my diary, which does not guarantee that I do not forget them.

Praying for people on the telephone can have problems when too many people 'phone up asking for prayers - I have had three 'phone call interruptions from people wanting prayer since I started writing this page. So sometimes I simply stop answering for a bit when I have to get on with something else; which is not an entirely satisfactory solution. Needless to say, I myself also sometimes 'phone people asking for prayer. It can be good to ask God to keep down the number of incoming calls and to see to it that one gets the calls He wants one to answer. I have written down what I have concerning my 'phone experience and problems in the hope that something I have written may be of a little help to people with similar problems. Let us thank God for the telephone, despite the difficulties!

Many Christians are finding it fruitful to have a prayer partner. As the name would suggest, two Christians keep in close touch with each other, share their problems and blessings, and uphold each other in prayer. The phone will often be very important in this relationship. Some of these partnerships have gone on for many years. Of course there is nothing new about friends sharing and praying with each other, but now it often seems to be happening in a more conscious and methodical way, for example, arranging to meet weekly for prayer at a given time.

There are many excellent Christian movements which encourage intercession in all our churches. I have been impressed by the mainly Evangelical-Pentecostal groups which are praying for revival - Catholics would probably speak of praying for the conversion of our country or the world. Indeed there is an organisation called 'Pray for Revival' *(tel 0121 6433 5611)* which arranges national conferences and other things, to encourage prayer for this intention. It seems to me that such a movement is a sign of deep faith and commitment to Jesus' command to spread the Gospel, especially because one is not likely to see immediate or personal answers to one's prayers.

I have been greatly edified by the intercession at Holy Trinity, Brompton, London, which is the mother church of the Alpha Course. As is well known, the Alpha

Course has been spreading very widely not only in this country but in many others, and it has led to very many thousands of conversions. The Alpha Course is now, in the year 2000. being used in a considerable majority of the prisons in this country, and Dartmoor now has a special wing for Christians. The point I want to make here is that the extraordinary fruitfulness of the Alpha Course has been and is based on so much powerful intercession.

In his book, 'The Church on its Knees' *(HTB Publications 1998)*, Jeremy Jennings of the staff at HTB describes the intercessory ministry there. This includes their early morning hour-long prayer meetings most days, their all-night prayer vigils, and their annual Prayer Weekends with about 170 people. They have also had the novel idea of hiring from time to time a boat on the Thames for about 300 people, to pray before different important centres like the House of Commons, and Westminster Abbey. Prayer for revival is one of their main themes of intercession. I remember once when I was at their Sunday evening service we all prayed for the conversion of Japan for about ten minutes, Japan being one of the most difficult areas for Christian missions. There is also much intercession in the many home groups linked with Holy Trinity, Brompton. It is difficult not to be impressed by their great confidence in the power of prayer and their dedication to intercession.

In the Catholic tradition intercession is often linked with the Eucharist - my own prayer intercession is centred round the celebration of the Eucharist. If Catholics are specially concerned about something such as an operation on a member of their family, a marriage in danger of breaking up, an interview which may result in redundancy, a spiritual crisis, they may well go to one or more weekday Masses to pray especially for the intention in question. Catholics will often pop into a church to say a prayer before the Eucharist in connection with a special need, whether the need is personal or wide such as peace in connection with Ireland.

I am impressed by the considerable number of Catholics who normally attend Mass daily, and I think this practice is in general a great source of intercession and spiritual strength. In our Benedictine parish here, where we have the advantage of being able to have these Masses every weekday and four on Sunday, because we have more priests, we normally have in total about 1,200 people at the Sunday Masses and over 100 on each weekday.

Obviously daily Mass is not possible for many people with jobs, or a busy study programme, or travelling problems, though they might manage to get to Mass on one or more days in the week. Retired people however can often go to daily Mass and this practice frequently seems to greatly enrich their lives and intercession. Some Christians reading these paragraphs may like to reflect on whether god is calling them to a more frequent participation in the Eucharist. However it is important to add that we must not become slaves to routine, and I am certainly not saying that God is calling every Catholic to daily Mass if that is possible - perhaps God is calling them to pray in other ways. Daily Mass is not an ancient practice in the Church. The early Benedictine monks, for example, only celebrated the Eucharist on Sundays and special feast days. Some people feel that the Mass is something too important to participate in daily. However, I should like to record that my own practice of daily Mass for 63 years has been a great source of wonderful blessings in many ways, including that of intercession.

For many Catholics the rosary, which I normally say daily, plays a very important part in their intercessions. They may offer up one or more decades of the rosary for this or that intention. There are, needless to say, many other devotions in the Catholic Church, for example Benediction of the Blessed Sacrament, the Way of the Cross, Litanies, Novenas. Something which seems to be helping many Christians in these years is the Devotion to the Divine Mercy Connected with a Polish sister, Blessed Faustina, who died in 1938. Although I do not say the special prayers normally connected with this devotion, I do find it a very real spiritual help. Are we individually and the Church and the world as a whole not so very obviously dependent on the Divine Mercy of Jesus, perhaps especially in the times in which we live? So calling on the Divine Mercy for ourselves and others is surely a vital form of intercession.

A warning: If readers tried to take on too many of the practices and devotions mentioned in this chapter they would suffer from spiritual indigestion. Each of us simply needs to ask the Holy Spirit to show us which are the practices and devotions for us and which are not for us. We should not feel that we ought to take on things because other people find them helpful, nor should we try to impose our own practices and devotions on others. For instance, I personally have been, and am very greatly blessed by, attending charismatic prayer meetings, but I know that these meetings are not for everyone, although I think, many more people could be greatly helped by them.

Some readers may object that a few of the practices and devotions which I have mentioned are not to be encouraged, since they are less 'sound' than others. I think we have to be very careful about judging how other people should pray. For me the key test is what in fact helps someone to pray well or better. For instance, though I personally would never recommend people to say the rosary during Mass, yet if that is what someone finds most prayerful, who am I to tell them that they should not be doing it? Let us leave the Holy Spirit to be the spiritual guide. Pray as best you can and not as other people think you should be praying. We can make suggestions as to what they may find helpful, like using a missal in Mass, but then let us leave them to pray as they find most fruitful.

One intercession which I would very much encourage is "Come Holy Spirit", or if one prefers asking the Father or Jesus to send the Holy Spirit. In recent years the prayer "Come, Holy Spirit" has been increasingly often on my lips and in my heart, and it means more and more to me. It is a prayer which I say for myself, for others, for the Church and for the world and I know I should pray it far more often than I do.

We are totally dependent on the Holy Spirit for the gift of faith and for an increase in faith. We are also dependent on the Holy Spirit for an understanding of our faith and of the Bible and of the teaching of the Church. A clever person could doubtless take a degree in Catholic theology while believing none of it, even being an atheist, by just learning the answers from a book. We need the light of the Holy Spirit for understanding people and situations. No amount of natural intelligence or learning, valuable as these can be, are a substitute for the illumination of the Holy Spirit.

We need the love of the Holy Spirit to fill us with love for God and for our neighbour. **If the Holy Spirit does not touch our hearts we will be God's *frozen* people rather than His *chosen* people.**

One of the hymns of the Divine Office (Prayer During the Day) prays: "Come Holy Spirit, live in us ...... and may that love within our hearts set fire to others with its flame." Without the love of the Holy Spirit "within our hearts" we shall not be able to play our part in spreading the gospel, "setting fire to others".

We need the strength and healing of the Holy Spirit. As the weak disciples were transformed at Pentecost into the fearless witnesses and martyrs which they became, we also need the strength of the Holy Spirit to carry our cross, and face any trials the Lord asks us to face.

I often pray, "come Holy Spirit, that I may bear fruit", or even "much fruit". Jesus wants each one of us not only to bear fruit for His Kingdom but to bear much fruit: "Those who abide in me and I in them bear much fruit .... My Father is glorified by this that you bear much fruit and become my disciples" *(John 15:5 & 8)*. We are all called to abide in Him and to be His disciples, so we are all called to bear 'much fruit', however much we have sinned in the past and whatever our personal limitations or the limitations of our situation. The Holy Spirit will give us all the grace and gifts to 'bear much fruit', if we ask Him. It may of course be a very hidden fruit like bearing the trial of blindness or Alzheimer's disease. But that does not make it less fruitful.

The ongoing repetition of some Christian phrase or prayer seems to be a form of prayer which an increasing number of Christians are finding helpful. An especially well-known example of that is the Jesus Prayer, associated with the tradition of the Eastern Christian monks. A common form of it is "Jesus have mercy on me, a sinner", which I find helpful to repeat for a time in my morning prayer and when I am having to fight anger. Another phrase often used is "Maranatha" ("Come, Lord Jesus") *(I Corinthians 16:22)* which is frequently recommended by the Christian Meditation Centre, associated with the names of the late Dom John Main OSB, and his successor Dom Lawrence Freeman OSB. *(address: The Priory of Christ the King, 29 Bramley Road, London N14 4HE).*

Fasting

Jesus said: "The days will come, when the bridegroom is taken away from them, and then they will fast" *(Matthew 9:15, Mark 2:18, and Luke 5:33).* In Matthew 6:16 Jesus says, "And *when* you fast", not *if* you fast. Jesus supposed that his disciples would fast from food.

Many Christians have found that in general when they added fasting to prayer there were more answers to prayer. Fasting seems often to add power to intercession. Of course fasting does not mean that our prayers are always answered as we first hoped. However, following the biblical injunction to fast does make a difference to our life of intercession. I want to say straight away that I am not in favour of any fasting which a doctor would not be happy about. So I am not in favour of abstaining from all liquids. But in general doctors would be very happy if more people fasted - it could improve their health.

So if you have some difficult problems in life try adding fasting to your prayer. Indeed, try fasting as a spiritual discipline in any case. Perhaps start by something small like giving up sugar in your tea and coffee or for a time alcohol. Or try simply dropping a meal from time to time. This could develop into going for a day without solid food, and then perhaps more than a day, but that is not for everyone.

We need not be frightened at the idea of a little fasting, adapted to our circumstances. Ask God to show you what, if anything, He wants you to do about fasting from food and to be given the grace and strength to do it. If we do that I am sure that many of us including myself, will do something, or something more, in the way of fasting, and our intercessions will increase in power. We can pray that we eat and drink all that God wants us to eat and drink - and only that. Any money saved in this way can be given to the hungry people of the world. Surely there is something very wrong when a large part of the world has the problem of not enough to eat, and another part has the problem of over-eating.

Lack of faith is sometimes a cause of prayer not being answered. When the disciples asked Jesus why they could not cure the epileptic boy He replied, "Because of your little faith" *(Luke 17:20).* Jesus at times complained of the lack of faith of his disciples, for example, when the boat was in a storm on the lake of Galilee and Jesus rebuked the storm, He said "Why are you afraid? Have you still no faith?" *(Mark 4:40)*. And in his teaching on material needs and the lilies of the field, He complains "you of little faith" *(Matthew 6:30)*. Jesus also commended the faith of some who were healed, for example, the woman with the haemorrhage, "your faith has made you well" *(Matthew 9:22)*.

I am not wishing to suggest that if we believe sufficiently strongly our prayers will always be answered in the way we first hoped - we cannot bend God's arm to do things He does not want to do. But in general if we had more faith we would see more answers to prayer.

I personally feel the need to repent increasingly of my lack of faith, hope, and trust in God, and to ask for greater gifts of faith, hope and trust. I am also much impressed by the example of those Christians who are really living by faith, who pray with great faith, and see beautiful answers to prayer. Perhaps many of us need more frequently to say with the apostles, "Increase our faith!" *(Luke 17:5)*.

It so happens that this morning a Catholic man who is taking a second degree in theology told me that one of his Catholic tutors with two doctorates assured him that "God does not intervene in answer to prayer like that. Things do not happen that way". A very learned priest lecturing in the same faculty takes the same line. I think we really have to face up to the fact that there is a real crisis of faith in some academic circles in the Catholic Church - and indeed in some other churches also - and that teaching of this kind helps to destroy or weaken the faith of many. Let us pray for these teachers who have lost their way and are leading others astray.

If Christians do not believe that God intervenes in answer to prayer then, so it seems to me, they have moved very far away from biblical Christianity and from historical Christian tradition, be it Catholic, Orthodox, Anglican, Protestant or Pentecostal. What sense do they make of saying the Our Father with its petitions? For me this is not something of secondary importance, but something vital and central to New Testament Christian living.

All Christians are called to intercede, and most of us should doubtless intercede much more than we do. The saints in all our churches were strong intercessors. Had they got it wrong? But many Christians find it difficult to concentrate all that much on intercession, because of other demands on time and energy. However, some Christians are called to a special ministry of intercession, that is to say that intercession is the main or a very important part of their service of God and human beings.

There are people who have quite a lot of time on their hands which could be used for prayer. This obviously applies to many sick or elderly Christians, but also to the unemployed, those who have retired, and to many people who live on their own. I think that God quite often gives such people a special vocation to intercession. This call can turn a life of frustration, boredom and meaninglessness into a life of great fruitfulness and fulfilment. I remember reading an account of someone who was very paralysed and could only communicate by pushing a button with her finger. Someone asked her, "Are you not bored just lying there all day and night, not able to move or speak"? She replied, "No, I am far too busy praying".

In my ministry I meet quite a number of people who used to be living a fruitful active life and now because of age or sickness or for other reasons cannot actively be as helpful as they used to be. Indeed, not only can they not help actively, but they are becoming an increasing burden to others, perhaps their spouse or children. This can lead to depression and to the feeling that it would be better if they were 'gone' - indeed, it can lead to suicide.

It may be very important to try to show such people that their lives can be wonderfully fruitful and meaningful through intercession, and through simply loving the people around them - right up to the last day in the geriatric ward. Now, I am a great believer in praying for healing and protection, but we shall not always be physically healed in this life - thank God, for otherwise we would never get to heaven!

Acceptance and offering up can be a very important part of our life and ministry of intercession. St Paul wrote: "I am now rejoicing in my sufferings for your sake, and in my flesh I am completing what is lacking in Christ's afflictions for the sake of His body, that is, the Church" *(Colossians 1:24)*. Yes, normally pray for healing and protection, but what is not healed or protected at one level can be wonderfully fruitful if accepted and offered up.

I advise people to ask God to show them for what intentions He wants them to offer up their life, their death, their joys, and their sufferings before the crisis comes. It may, for example, be for my family and peace and justice in Ireland. None of us knows when we may be hit by a car, a mugger, a heart attack or by germs.

Think about it all, and offer it up before you are hit by the car, or whatever, so that it is all taken up in your intercessory prayer. In that way your life can be truly, indeed wonderfully, fruitful and meaningful whatever happens.

When shall we have finished our service of intercession? When we die? In the Catholic tradition we believe that the saints in heaven pray for us, and indeed we ask for their prayers. Are we only thinking of outstanding canonised saints? Certainly not. So you can ask your devout departed grandmother to pray for you. Every day I say a general prayer for the departed members of my family, that they may rest in peace and I ask them to pray for me and for the other living members of our family.

The saints in heaven help us through their prayer. St Thérèsa of Lisieux said that when she got to heaven she would send down a shower of roses through her prayers to help people on earth. Padre Pio has appeared from heaven to heal not a few people through his prayer - I spoke to one of them who was dying when Padre Pio appeared. He knew nothing about Padre Pio and only recognised who it was from a photo later. (His testimony is being used for the canonisation). But it is not only great saints who help from above. In any case, who can decide who are the 'great' saints and who are the others? I have met many Christians who were convinced that they were being helped by departed mothers, fathers, spouses or other people. So we ordinary Christians can hope that when by the grace of God we get to heaven He will use our prayers to help people on earth. There is surely every reason that a mother who is praying for a sick or needy child on earth will continue to pray for the child after she herself dies. So your ministry of intercession will continue after your death - and perhaps be more powerful then. Alleluia.

One last, but very important point in connection with intercession. **As far as possible, our intercessions should be linked with, surrounded by, and shot through with praise and thanksgiving.....** but that brings us to the next chapter, on praise.

Chapter Eight
Praise

In this chapter I am writing not only on praise but also about thanksgiving and adoration, because in practice these three tend to run into each other. We thank God for what He has done for us, we praise Him for what He is in Himself, and we adore Him out of love.

When I realised the next chapter of this book should be on praise, I found that I had hesitations. I asked myself how am I doing in my life in the area of praise and thanksgiving these days, and I felt the answer was "not so good". So I found myself thinking that perhaps I ought to brush up my praise and thanksgiving for a time before writing about them. On reflection, I realised that would be hypocritical. It would be more honest to show myself as I really am, a Christian who is continually struggling to give praise its rightful place in his life rather than as someone who is riding along on a cloud of praise. So I am also writing this chapter for my own benefit!

Many of us find, I think, that we tend to spend too much of our prayer time in asking for things and not enough in praising and thanking God. We are of course quite right to be asking for things - we should probably be doing far more asking than we do, as I showed in the last chapter. However, our asking should be surrounded by, permeated and shot through with, praise and thanksgiving and that is often where we fail, where I fail.

This can result in our intercession becoming something of an anxious worrying rather than hopeful prayer. And we can easily become problem centred and then often self-centred rather than Jesus-centred, God-centred. For example, praying for one's financial needs or health problems can easily drift into just worrying about finances and health.

So if someone is praying about financial needs it could be good to start by thanking God for His provision in the past and to thank Him for the material things one already has. If praying for health one can thank God for the health one has, for being able to hear, see and walk if one can do these things. If one is praying for peace and justice in connection with Ireland or Yugoslavia one can begin by thanking God for the progress made in the peace talks and thank Him for all the good people who are truly working for peace.

It is helpful to remind ourselves that when Jesus taught us to pray He started with praise, "Hallowed by Thy name". Before we ask that His perfect will be done in us, that He will provide for our needs, that He will forgive us, that He will protect us, we praise His holy name. How often do I in fact praise and thank before asking for things? In 1 Peter 2:9 we read: " But you are a chosen race, a royal priesthood, a consecrated nation, a people set apart to sing the praises of God". That is also something for now, not just for Heaven. Ask yourself how much praising you have done in the last two days, the last week. Are you in truth someone who in reality is living up to your vocation to "sing the praises of God"? Note that this vocation to praise is not just something for contemplative nuns and monks but for all Christians, although of course this vocation will be lived by busy lay people in a different way to nuns and monks. One can add that the fact that one is living a monastic life and spending quite a lot of time in monastic offices does not at all guarantee that one is living a true life of praise and thanksgiving interiorly - I know from my own personal experience!

The psalms also remind us of our vocation to praise. For example, psalm 145 starts: "I will extol you, my God and King, and bless your name forever. Every day I will bless you, and praise your name for ever and ever. Great is the Lord, and greatly to be praised; his greatness is unsearchable". The prefaces of the Mass also take up the themes of praise and thanksgiving. For example, take the preface of the second Eucharistic Prayer: "Father it is our duty and our salvation, always and everywhere to give you thanks through your beloved Son, Jesus Christ ...... And so we join the angels and saints in proclaiming your glory. Hosanna in the highest. Blessed is he who comes in the name of the Lord. Hosanna in the highest".

Indeed the whole Mass is primarily a prayer of praise and thanksgiving. The word Eucharist means thanksgiving. Some of us, and I include myself, can at times be in danger of seeing the Mass primarily as an occasion to ask God for things, which is of course a very important element in the Mass, rather than as primarily a prayer of thanksgiving and praise. And the liturgy of the Divine Office, which is not only a prayer for monks, priests and religious, is centred on the theme of praise.

However, it is not always easy to praise and thank God, indeed it is sometimes totally impossible to do so without a special grace from God. If a person is extremely depressed, if someone's husband has just dropped down dead unexpectedly leaving the wife and four children, if one has just been blinded in a car crash, if all one's material security has suddenly vanished in old age through the dishonesty of someone else, if unexpectedly you discover that your daughter is a serious heroin addict - the list could easily be continued - probably the last thing you would feel like doing is praising and thanking God. Indeed, you might well be feeling very angry with God for having allowed these things to happen. Why me, why us?

Praising and thanking God, however, are not basically a matter of the feelings but of the will. By the grace of God we can often simply decide to praise and thank Him and then do so whatever our feelings. As has often been said, we sometimes have to praise God through gritted teeth. However, we must be careful not to urge people to praise God when it is not the right moment for them. If I were badly hurt in a car crash perhaps the only prayer I could manage would be "Jesus help me" - indeed I might well not manage a prayer at all. We need to remember that Jesus was not carried along on a cloud of praise in Gethsemanie, and that we may well have our Gethsemanie moments when the most that God may be asking of us will be to say "not my will but yours be done" *(Luke 22:42).*

Yet it remains true that we often need to praise and thank God when we are not feeling like it, and that we should seek to develop the practice, with God's grace, of praising and thanking Him in the difficult times. It may help us to see the importance of this if we remember that praise and thanksgiving are an important part of loving

God, and that we are called to fulfil the first commandment of loving God not just when things are going well. I personally find that I often do more praising of God when I am in trouble than when things are going well. Indeed I sometimes wonder whether at times God allows me to get into difficulties because He wants me to praise Him more!

To give an example, a few years ago I was attending an international conference on praying for healing in San Giovanni Rotondo, where Blessed Padre Pio lived. The afternoon before we had to leave for England, I could not find my return air ticket. The situation was complicated by the fact that I had to transfer quickly from one hotel to another two days earlier. I looked very thoroughly for the ticket in my baggage, but in vain. So I handed the problem over to Jesus and spent the next two lectures praising Him instead of listening. Then I looked again for the ticket and found it in my dirty linen! The two hours when the ticket was lost was the time when I did the most intense praising during my whole stay there.

This story underlines another point. Praise often seems to release the power of Jesus, of God, into a situation in a new way. Quite often when there is authentic praise, especially powerful praise, remarkable things happen. Merlin Carothers in his books Prison to Praise and Power in Praise gives examples of very wonderful healings and other remarkable things happening when people really gave themselves to praise. However, it is important to add that praise must not be an attempt to bend God's arm to do things He does not want to do, such as healing a particular person's cancer, when God wants to take that person to heaven. We must praise whether someone is healed or not, whether someone passes an exam or not, whether she says yes to a proposal of marriage or not. Our praise must be based on an acceptance of God's perfect will in every circumstance, trusting God that He knows what is best in every situation and trusting that He will always bring good out of evil if we let Him. As we read in Isaiah 55:8, "For my thoughts are not your thoughts, nor are your ways my ways, says the Lord. For as the heavens are higher than the earth, so are my ways higher than your ways and my thoughts higher than your thoughts".

Moreover, as far as we can we should praise and thank Jesus, God, for the situation in which we find ourselves, including its difficulties and even its horrors. Our present situation is where God has put or allowed us to be, and our present situation is His opportunity for doing in one way or another something beautiful in our lives. So if I were in prison for peddling drugs, I could thank God for that situation. I would not thank Him that I had sinned by peddling drugs - I should repent of that - but I could thank Him that God will bring good out of that evil if I let him. Indeed to take an actual case, Sr Breige McKenna tells of how a drug addict in Singapore who was converted through her ministry was used to convert a whole group of addicts in prison before they were all executed.

In my own life as a priest-monk I went through a very difficult period of depression, which at the time prevented me from getting on with my ministry and which seemed nothing but a disaster out of which no good could come. But my healing ministry of prayer, such as it is, was born in that difficult time of darkness.

So now I can thank God for that suffering period and the good He has brought out of it. I am not saying that God sent me that depression, I would think rather that the devil was involved with it. But God upheld me in it and brought good out of it.

St Paul wrote: "We know that all things work together for good for those who love God" *(Romans 8:28)*. We need to pray for the grace to believe this, especially in the difficult times. As we believe this we shall find it easier to give ourselves to praising and thanking God in difficult situations.

When I lose or mislay something I start by looking for it, then I ask Jesus to help me to find it, then I begin to praise Jesus. So often it is only when I praise Him that I find the lost object. Once, however I lost the crown of a tooth which I had carefully put aside, and I could not find it despite all the looking and praising. Later the dentist told me that the roots of the tooth were in fact no longer strong enough to support the crown, and that it was in fact fortunate that I had lost the crown. Then I thanked God for not answering my prayer to find the lost crown!

I am aware of course that things like finding the lost crown of a tooth, or one's glasses are relatively very small matters in a world in which so many people are having to face great problems and sufferings. However, if we learn to praise and thank God in the face of smaller problems that will prepare us for doing so when great trials come along. If we experience the loving care of God in small things, that will increase our faith for facing the big trials. And when we praise and thank God in the face of big difficulties and trials we shall in fact often, but not always, experience that the objective situation has improved.

What can we do practically to praise and thank God, Jesus more? Going to Mass more often can be a big help, for Mass is the supreme form of worship, praise and thanks giving. Praying regularly some of the Divine Office may help some people to praise more. But participating in liturgical services does not automatically result in authentic interior praise and thanksgiving, although it normally helps. In our times many Christians involved in the Charismatic Renewal, including myself, have found that praying with the gift of tongues has greatly helped them to praise and thank God, but doubtless the gift of tongues is not for every Christian.

I think that many Christians are finding that spontaneous prayer as the Holy Spirit leads them helps them to praise better, indeed helps their prayer in other ways also. So someone can simply say, "Thank you Jesus" or "Thank you God" for this beautiful weather, for a safe journey, for my family, for my boss, for helping me to stop smoking, for answering my prayer, for the Holy Eucharist, for saving me - the list could obviously go on. Someone might simply feel led to go on repeating "Thank you Jesus" or "Thank you God" for quite a time. I think it will often help us to thank and praise if we stop to count our blessings, especially if we do this when things are difficult. If you are worrying about the health of your lungs, thank God for all the parts of your body which are functioning well. Count your blessings. Remember all the obvious blessings in your life like a happy marriage, and thank God for them. Thank God for the gifts and talents He has given you. (There are so many blessings we simply take for granted like being able to see or hear, until they are threatened or lost). I find myself increasingly thanking God for my beloved parents and for other departed members of my family. How much I have received through them! We should thank God for all the natural blessings He has given us, but we should do so even more for the spiritual blessings. Thank God that He created us out of love, thank Jesus for having suffered and died for our salvation, thank the Holy Spirit for dwelling within us and for His gifts. Give thanks for the sacraments of the Church, for the Bible, for the support of the prayers of others, for our spiritual mother Mary, for the saints, and angels. And thank Jesus for a share in His sufferings, which is more difficult. St Paul wrote: "I am now rejoicing in my sufferings for your sake, and in my flesh I am completing what is lacking in Christ's afflictions for the sake of his body, that is, the Church". *(Colossians 1:24)*.

Each one of us will find that different things particularly inspire us to thanks and praise. I personally find that the beauty of nature and flowers frequently helps me to praise and thank God the Father who created them.

I am writing this chapter on praise while spending a week with my sister and her husband, who have a lovely garden in beautiful country near the Lake District. For me this is a wonderful setting for writing on praise. Other people will be especially helped by music, still others by the wonders revealed by scientific study. And we can all, I hope, be moved to thanksgiving by the goodness of some human beings. Watching the funeral of Cardinal Hume on television yesterday inspired me and many others to thank God for his life.

Each one of us will find different ways to help us to praise more. I often try to praise Jesus when I am walking up stairs, which I do frequently in our monastery. I probably forget to do this more often than not. But this practice does help to give praise a greater place in my life. I think it is important to seek to give praise and thanksgiving a regular place - and not too short a one - in our daily routine of prayer. The liturgy can be a great help there, but not everyone is able to participate daily in the liturgy. Grace before and after meals is surely a helpful practice. Before I turn the light out at night I try to thank God for the day and its blessings. (You will notice that here and elsewhere I write "try to". Being a rather distracted person at 78, I frequently forget to do things like saying grace after meals. This however does not worry me too much. God knows what I am like! So I just try to do better in the future).

In the Catholic Church adoration is frequently linked with the Mass and the Blessed Sacrament. Devotion to Jesus in the Blessed Sacrament, having diminished somewhat after the Second Vatican Council, is now on the increase again, and I think this is bearing much spiritual fruit. Just kneeling or sitting before the tabernacle or the Blessed Sacrament exposed is obviously helping many people, as we find in movements like Youth 2000, Cor Lumen Christi, and the groups connected with Charles de Foucauld. Many people visit the chapel of the Benedictine nuns at Tyburn in London where the Blessed Sacrament is exposed day and night. Just being there in silence in front of the Blessed Sacrament can open people up to a more contemplative dimension of prayer, where stillness and silence largely replaces words.

Praise can be very important in praying for healing. It is not for nothing that healing services usually start with a quite lengthy period of praise. The healings of spirits, minds and bodies which do or do not take place can be closely linked with the depth of the praise. I once saw a sick foot being progressively healed over about twenty minutes while the two members of the healing team who were ministering to the lady simply went on praising fervently. Indeed in Christian gatherings where the praise is really intense, sometimes healings of spirits, minds, and bodies take place without anyone having explicitly prayed for healing for the particular illnesses in question.

Praise can also be very important in spiritual warfare. The devil does not like hearing Jesus being praised. Fervent praise can not only protect people from demonic attacks, it can also liberate them from demonic troubles. If an individual, a family, a prayer group or a parish really keeps authentic praise flowing, that can be a great help in the spiritual warfare in which we are all involved.

There is, I think, a close connection between praise and joy. How often have I gone to a prayer meeting or a liturgical service feeling heavy and perhaps discouraged, to find that after a period of real praise, the feeling of heaviness and discouragement has gone. The same could apply to praising and thanking God on my own.

Joy and peace seem to be closely linked with praise and thanksgiving. The words of St Paul to the Philippians seem very relevant here: "Rejoice in the Lord always; again I say, rejoice. Let your gentleness be known to everyone. The Lord is near. Do not worry about anything, but in everything by prayer and supplication with thanksgiving let your requests be made known to God. And the peace of God, which surpasses all understanding, will guard your hearts and your minds in Christ Jesus" *(Philippians 4:4-7)*.

In this chapter I have written of things which may, I hope, help some readers to praise and thank God better. However, all the suggestions in the world will make no difference unless Jesus Himself touches our minds and hearts. We cannot force ourselves to praise and thank authentically. It is all a matter of His grace and mercy. We can however, ask for the grace to praise and thank, for the grace to do these things more truly, more fully. Let us ask for the grace to do that until the 'day' comes when through His mercy our faltering praise will be perfected in the heavenly choir above. *Alleluia*.

Chapter Nine
Contemplation

Modern Catholic spiritual writers increasingly say, and I think rightly so, that all Christians are called to contemplation. This does not mean that every Christian will or should experience special gifts of contemplation. I think it means that there should be, indeed will be, a contemplative element or dimension in every mature life of prayer, although some Christians are temperamentally more inclined in a contemplative direction than others.

There is a difference between the reflective meditation on Jesus, on God, and the contemplative awareness of the presence of Jesus, of God. Reflective meditation has an important part to play in the life of prayer. We need to meditate on the Bible and on the life of Jesus in the New Testament. In our life in this world we shall never get beyond the need to meditate on the life of Jesus and the Bible. However, in reflective meditation we are intellectually thinking about Jesus, whereas in contemplation we are in some way experiencing the presence of Jesus. We are called not only to know *about* Jesus, but in some way to *know* Jesus. The 'head' knowledge of Jesus, of God, is important, but we are called to go beyond that and to have a 'heart' knowledge. We are called to know through love, indeed if there is no love there will be no truly living knowledge of Jesus, of God.

Needless to say, Christians should not make contemplative experience or special contemplative graces their aim in the Christian life. That could lead to all sorts of self seeking, spiritual pride, and illusions. Our fundamental aim must surely be to grow in the first two commandments of loving God and our neighbour. It is as we grow in love that we shall open ourselves to authentic spiritual experience. St Teresa of Avila valued true ecstasy because it can lead to a great increase in love. That surely is a key test for all mystical experiences. Are they in fact making the recipient a more loving person? Contemplative experience may not always take the form of experiencing light, as we read in the lives of some of the saints who experienced great darkness. There is a long tradition of having to pass through periods of aridity, the desert, and dark nights in the spiritual life, and these times can be important periods of purification, growth, and testing. Are we seeking the consolations of God rather than God Himself? However, I must admit to sometimes being rather worried at what I feel can become something of a cult of darkness, which suggests that the more darkness the better, that darkness is the normal state of prayer, or that darkness is the safest way.

Jesus said: "I am the light of the world. Whoever follows me will never walk in darkness but will have the light of life" *(John 8:12)*. The many references to light in the New Testament are nearly always referring to something spiritually positive, and the references to darkness nearly always to something spiritually negative. For example: "Whoever loves a brother or sister lives in the light, and in such a person there is no cause for stumbling. But whoever hates another brother or sister is in the darkness, walks in the darkness, and does not know the way to go, because the darkness has brought on blindness" *(I John 2:10).*

So, although it is important not to misunderstand, and criticise Christians who are going through dark nights and arid periods in prayer - indeed we should know how to help and support them - I think we should basically maintain the New Testament perspective of light. Indeed, the dark nights of St John of the Cross are preparing us for an even fuller experience of light - in this life or in the next.

I have the impression, and many others would agree, that in these times God is being especially generous with His contemplative and mystical graces in the lives of many Christians. I seem to meet or hear of an increasing number of Christians who are having special contemplative experiences of the presence of Jesus, of God, or perhaps of Mary. Or perhaps they are experiencing visions, touches or messages. And it is not only among Pentecostal or Charismatic Christians that these things are happening. Of course some of these experiences may not be authentic, do not come from God. Mental illness, emotional stress, or demonic forces can all play their part in creating illusions. There could also sometimes be straightforward fraud. Obviously it is necessary to try to discern carefully whether or not these experiences come from God, as I have tried to explain in Chapter 5 on Listening to God. And it is not just a question of black or white. There can sometimes be grey areas. The right question can be, how far something is of God. Even the visions and messages of the canonised saints are not infallible.

However, I know of apostolic initiatives which have

the blessing of the bishop and have been very fruitful for years, which were set in motion by a special mystical grace or word from the Lord. Special guidance did not stop with the Acts of the Apostles, as we can see from reading the lives of many of the canonised saints. At a much humbler level, I myself was protected from taking a wrong path in my ministry by a clear and repeated "No" from the Lord. The course of action in question, which at the time seemed the obvious thing to do, would in any case have had to receive the permission of my monastic superiors. However, I never got as far as asking for permission on account of the repeated interior "No" I was receiving. Looking back on the whole question over ten years later, I can see how right God's "No" was, although at the time I could not understand it.

Visions and words from God are not only for holy people. I remember talking with a lady who earlier in life had a vision of an angel. That did not stop her later going off the rails. However, when I spoke to her still later in life, she said that it was because of the vision of the angel she had sold some land to the church when she could have got a higher price elsewhere, and she attributed her coming back to the church and Christianity to the memory of that earlier vision of the angel. I think there is every reason to believe that particular vision of an angel was authentic.

Some people assume that any mystical experience or word from the Lord must be inauthentic if the person in question suffers from any mental illness. I would disagree with that. I think that God sometimes gives someone a special grace because their need is so great. I have known well for about fifteen years a woman who had experienced a very severe mental collapse. She is now, thank God, considerably better, indeed one psychiatrist tells her that she is medically speaking a 'success story', even though her life is still difficult. The lady in question received during her illness two or three significant touches or experiences from the Lord in one way or another. I think that it was because of those special experiences that she persevered in prayer through the very difficult years. I think that without those special experiences or something similar she would have given up prayer and probably committed suicide.

"You will know them by their fruits" *(Matthew 7:16)*. If mystical experiences and words form the Lord lead to greater faith, hope and love - and to greater fruitfulness in life, then there is reason to believe that they are basically authentic. That would not necessarily rule out all possibility of some error. However, I meet or hear of so many Christians who have obviously been blessed through their special contemplative or mystical experiences that I cannot doubt that these experiences were often at least basically from God. The same would apply to the many fruits of the Christian healing ministry of prayer.

There seems to be a division of the Christian world between those Christians who believe that authentic special contemplative and mystical experiences coming from the Lord still happen, and those very liberal Christians who do not so believe, and who would seek to explain it all psychologically. Of course the official Catholic position is that miracles and mystical experiences still sometimes happen, but some Catholics have been very influenced - too influenced - by liberal Protestantism and the prevailing secular humanism of our times, which would explain all such experiences psychologically.

I would like to suggest that there is food for thought in the fact that in the Protestant world it is the Pentecostal and Charismatic evangelical churches which are in general flourishing and expanding, sometimes rapidly, and the liberal Protestant churches and milieu which are in general declining, sometimes dramatically. I would personally have reservations about some Pentecostal prophecy concerning the 'end times'. Indeed Pentecostals often disagree among themselves on that subject. However, I think that so many Catholics have yet to recognise the fact that we are living alongside the groups of Pentecostal type Christians who in one century have expanded from nothing to about four hundred million members, and that it is this group of Christians who are growing most quickly today. Moreover, their growth and vitality are clearly connected with what they would call 'supernatural' experiences coming from God. (Catholics and Pentecostals use the word 'supernatural' in different senses. For Catholic theology 'supernatural' means the whole realm of grace, while for Pentecostals and many evangelicals the word "supernatural" means extraordinary happenings like miracles and visions. In fact I think an increasing number of Catholics are now using this word in a Pentecostal and evangelical sense).

Of course as a convinced Catholic priest there are some other areas in which I would disagree with the Pentecostals, for example, I would find their eucharistic belief and practice inadequate. I would also find some

Pentecostals too narrow on the question of who is saved. This however does not stop me from recognising that the Holy Spirit is often working very strongly in the Pentecostal and charismatic churches, and I think that we Catholics have frequently something to learn from them, as they have from us. For example, have we Catholics not something to learn from the zeal for and dedication to evangelisation which we so often find in the Pentecostal and Charismatic churches?

Chapter Ten
Difficulties in Prayer

Prayer is a wonderful gift from God, a glorious adventure, and a great source of fruitfulness. But praying is not always easy, indeed it can be extremely difficult at times. Jesus was not on cloud nine when in his agony in Gethsemanie He prayed, "Father, if you are willing, remove this cup from me; yet, not my will but yours be done" *(Luke 22:42)*. In fact He sweated blood. So we must not be surprised if sometimes our prayer is difficult, even very difficult.

What are the reasons why prayer is sometimes difficult? There are various possible reasons, and at times they may combine. Ill health can be a cause. I have met many people who told me that prayer was very difficult when they had a bad attack of flu, and I cannot remember anyone who found prayer easy when they had serious flu. When illness is making prayer difficult we just have to pray as best we can. Long prayers will probably not be possible. Short phrases will probably be best, like "Help me, Jesus", "Heal me, Jesus" "Thy will be done", "Jesus, have mercy", "I offer it up", "Thank you, Jesus", "Alleluia" or just "Jesus".

Exhaustion and tiredness can make prayer difficult. It may be right when possible to cut down on our activity, so that we can pray more easily. Workaholics, please note!

Worldly preoccupations and ambition will affect our prayer. If people are making the pursuit of great wealth their main aim in life, then obviously they will not feel like praying or find true prayer meaningful. The same could apply to the pursuit of fame, power, or any other false God.

Serious sin which we have not repented of and which we are not making a real effort to overcome will clearly blunt the desire to pray. That could apply for example, to sexual promiscuity or serious involvement in the occult. People could find these two pursuits so absorbing that there is no time and energy left over for God. So if people are finding prayer difficult they could examine their lives to see whether they are worshipping false Gods.

Prayer can be difficult because we are trying to pray in a way which is not right for us, at least at the present time. For instance, trying to meditate discursively at length when God is calling someone to contemplation will not be helpful. Nor will rushing through liturgical offices just to fulfil an obligation. Nor will trying to pray through a particular private devotion which God is not calling one to be involved in. Nor will trying to pray at length at night if you keep falling asleep - we need if possible to pray at a time of day or night which is suitable for us, and that will vary from person to person.

Then there may be the times of aridity, the dark nights, the desert periods mentioned in the last chapter. The important thing is not to give up prayer, which is what the devil will try to persuade us to do. We just have to persevere gently as best we can until the Lord Himself brings us into the light.

There is another difficulty which perhaps I should mention. Drinking too much alcohol and overeating can make prayer difficult, while fasting can be a help to prayer.

A major problem in prayer can of course be distractions. Indeed, it is normal that we all experience distractions at times, perhaps even much of the time for a period in our life.

There are distractions for which we are at least in part responsible and those for which we are not directly. For example, if I spend the hour before Mass watching a violent film, then probably during Mass my mind will be invaded by the violent film. Indeed, much reading, TV, and radio can give rise to distractions and be unhelpful in prayer. Or if I unnecessarily go to bed too late - which happens too often - then that does not help my night prayers, which suffer from distractions.

However, there are times when we are trying to pray and all kinds of distractions just enter our minds for no obvious reason. They may just reflect our current preoccupations, worries and concerns. The best way, I think, of dealing with such distractions is often to turn them into prayer for the people and situations involved. Indeed, what we first see as just a distraction may sometimes be the Holy Spirit wanting to change the direction of our prayer. I may have wanted to pray at this Mass specially for one person, but God may be asking us to pray especially for someone else.

There can, however, be distractions which are caused by the devil playing on our weaknesses. Someone may find during his or her time of prayer that his or her mind is invaded by sinful thoughts, perhaps wrong anger, envy, self pity, lust or pride. When that happens we can ask Jesus to protect us from these attacks of the devil, or in the name of Jesus we can command the devil to leave us, as I explained in my book "I Saw Satan Fall: The Ways of Spiritual Warfare" *(chapter 6)*.

Some people find it helpful to have a notebook and biro at their side, so that they can jot down quickly things which need to be remembered. For example, if when you are praying you suddenly remember that it is important to phone someone this evening, then jot it down. Otherwise you may spend the rest of your prayer time thinking I must not forget that phone call this evening!

An important thing, I think, is not to be too upset by our distractions in prayer, for that itself can discourage us from praying. We should just bring our minds peacefully back to prayer, and continue praying.

If during my morning prayer time I feel that I really have got through to God, then I am not too worried by all the distraction involved on the way. God knows what our weak minds are like. He made us!

The important thing about the difficulties is not to let them discourage us from praying or trying to pray. Let us remember the story of the Widow and the Unjust Judge: "Then Jesus told them a parable about their need to pray and not to lose heart" *(Luke 18:1)*.

Epilogue

The purpose in writing this book has been to encourage everyone to have a greater conviction of the importance of prayer and hopefully to help them in their life of prayer. Many of the readers of this book are certainly better prayers than I am - it is humbling for someone who is a priest and monk to meet lay Christians who from experience obviously know much more about prayer than he does. I spoke with someone on the phone today who said that they have spent the last two days praying for a particular intention. Then there are my friends who stay up praying late into the night in prayer vigils, and those who regularly fast seriously. So who am I to write a book on prayer? Perhaps my excuse is that I am in touch with many Christians who really are great prayers. So I can pass on to others the fruits of their experience.

I do have a very deep conviction about the great importance of prayer. I see the way in which many people's lives have been wonderfully transformed through prayer. I also meet Christians from many church backgrounds whose lives are very fruitful through prayer, who regularly experience beautiful answers to prayer, perhaps especially in healing.

In a way prayer unites two aspects of my own life: the monastic-priestly side and the Charismatic Renewal side. I have met over the years some very deeply prayerful priests and monastics. I have also met some equally prayerful Christians involved in the Charismatic renewal. (And I also of course know some wonderfully prayerful men and women who do not come into either of those categories).

In this country and in not a few others Christianity is facing a crisis of falling numbers, and especially the loss of so many of the younger generation. The Tablet recently published a series of articles on the subject, "Where have all the Catholics gone?" *(starting 19th June 1999)*. Some other churches could have equally well published similar articles. The first article states that the only growing churches in our country are the 'Charismatic evangelicals'. I am not wanting to suggest that the only Christian groups which can grow are the charismatic ones. But I do think it is only the Christian groups which take prayer very seriously who will grow in our times.

On the international level it is in general in the Third World that Christianity is growing. Consider, for example, the very rapid increase of Christianity in South Korea and in China. In these countries the expanding Christianity is one in which there is much praying. One flourishing church in South Korea expects all its members to pray for an hour or two each day before work, and expects its pastors to pray for six hours daily. Surely that is the kind of ethos we see in the New Testament. As we return to the New Testament example of a deeply praying church we shall surely be moving towards the conversion of our world to Jesus.

Come Holy Spirit, help us to pray

I have written three appendices: 'Mary the Saints and the Angels', 'Charismatic Renewal', and 'The Gift of Tongues'. I have put these three sections as appendices because I hope the rest of the book will be accessible for all Christians. Obviously very many wonderful Christians are not happy with asking Mary to pray for us. Equally, many wonderful Christians do not feel drawn to Charismatic spirituality and the gift of tongues. However some people may like to read these sections just for information, just to see how some of their fellow Christians pray.

Appendix One
Mary, The Saints, and The Angels

Now I have come to what is for me the most difficult section of this book to write, the part which deals with Mary, the saints and the angels. Indeed I have been tempted simply to drop this appendix, but I feel that would not really be honest.

I am hoping that this book will be read not only by Catholics, but also by other Christians, including some Evangelicals and Pentecostals. Up to now they will, I hope, have felt basically at home with all I have written. That will no longer I fear, be the case with this appendix. However, I hope they will continue to read on, if only to see what Catholic minded Christians think on this subject. In an authentic ecumenism we must be willing to face up to our differences without pretending that they do not exist or fudging them.

Catholics ask Mary, the saints and the angels to pray for them to Jesus, to God, so do all the historic Eastern churches, and so do many Anglicans and a number of other Christians. Evangelicals and Pentecostal Christians do not. And why? Because they say that our religious beliefs and practices should be based on what is clearly written in the Bible, and there is nothing directly on this subject in the Bible.

Catholics reply that alongside Scripture there is Tradition as a source of belief and practice, and that the Catholic attitude towards this and some other subjects is justified by appealing to Tradition.

It is, I hope, obvious to all Christians that there are many very wonderful Christians with very deep and powerful prayer lives who have never asked Mary, the saints, or angels to pray for them or for anyone else. So these practices are clearly not necessary in order to have a very profound life of Christian prayer, which of course has to be centred on Jesus. We also need to remember that "there is only one mediator between God and humankind, Christ Jesus, himself human, who gave himself as a ransom for all" *(I Timothy 2:5)*. Nobody is saved except through Jesus. Indeed, Jesus is the saviour of His mother, Mary.

However, it would appear evident to many of us that very many Christian's prayer lives, while clearly centred on Jesus, have been enriched by asking especially Mary to pray with them and for them. Indeed, I myself am convinced that praying to and with Mary helps my spiritual life. I am convinced that my praying to Mary helps me to love and serve Jesus more. So I would not want to give it up because that would, I feel sure, reduce my love for Jesus.

For a number of years I was not particularly interested in going to Lourdes where Mary appeared to St Bernadette in 1858. The reason for this lukewarmness was partly because I was much involved in ecumenical work with Christians linked with the Reformation, and I did not feel that visiting shrines of Our Lady went particularly well with such ecumenical work. However, I found myself leading a charismatic pilgrimage to Lourdes about fifteen years ago and have done so almost annually ever since. The point I want to make here is that our pilgrimages to Lourdes have, I am totally convinced, increased the place of Jesus in our lives, not diminished it. I also want to say here that I personally am convinced that Mary is appearing in our times in Medjugorje and in quite a number of other places, and that these apparitions are bearing much fruit for Jesus.

I know of course that there are sometimes false apparitions and exaggerations in Marian devotion, and papal documents have warned Catholics against such exaggerations. I myself am not entirely happy with pictorial representations which appear to put Mary on the same level as Jesus. Nor am I happy with writings which say much about God the Father and Mary, while saying practically nothing about Jesus. We Catholics would sometimes seem to go out of our way to make it more difficult for evangelicals and Pentecostals and many other Christians to understand the true Catholic attitude towards Mary. Moreover, Mary herself is not pleased when we exaggerate her role. She wants the focus to be on Jesus not on herself, Mary always points us to her Son.

We Catholics ask Mary, the saints and the angels to pray with us and for us. What we are doing is basically the same as when we ask another living person to pray for us. The difference between us and the Evangelicals is that we believe that we can still ask someone to pray for us after their death and Evangelicals do not. The blessings and graces received after such prayer come from Jesus, God, not from the human person who prayed living or departed. (In Medjugorje Mary once said to one of the visionaries that it was Jesus who healed, not her).

Having clarified, I hope, the basic position, I must add

that I think it should be normal for a Catholic to have a very real devotion to Mary. The Holy Spirit will inspire some Catholics to go further in that direction than others. However, I think there is something missing in a Catholic's life of prayer if Mary is neglected. Mary, my heavenly mother, has a very important place in my life of prayer, but definitely secondary to Jesus, who is my only Saviour. And I think my devotion to Mary leads to Jesus, of course everything is summed up in God, Father, Son and Holy Spirit.

Some Catholics may think that in this section I have gone too far in seeking to avoid upsetting Evangelicals and Pentecostals. May I remind those Catholics that Pope John Paul II has made Christian unity one of the great intentions of the Millennium. Since Vatican II Christian unity and ecumenical dialogue have been officially a major concern of the Catholic Church. Obviously Catholics cannot sacrifice their essential beliefs for the sake of unity, any more than other Christians can.

Clearly the different attitudes of Christians towards Mary are an important cause of division among Christians. Let us pray for the day when Christians are united in their attitude towards Mary, the mother of Jesus. And let us try to help and not hinder the ecumenical dialogue on Mary. For those interested in this dialogue there is The Ecumenical Society of the Blessed Virgin Mary. (*address: 11 Belmont Road, Wallington, Surrey SM6 8TE*).

~~~~~~~~~

Catholic minded Christians not only pray with and to Mary, they also pray with and to the saints and angels, who are united with us in the Communion of Saints. When we think of the saints we are not only thinking of that almost infinitely small proportion of the saints who have been canonised. We are thinking of the multitude mentioned in Revelation chapter 7: "After this I looked, and there was a great multitude that no one could count, from every nation, from all tribes and peoples and languages, standing before the throne and before the Lord, robed in white with palm branches in their hands. They called out in a loud voice, saying, "Salvation belongs to our God who is seated on the throne, and to the Lord!"

Many Catholics will pray particularly with and to a canonised saint on their liturgical feast day, for example St Benedict on the 11th July, St Teresa of Lisieux on 1st October. It is fairly normal that a Catholic will have a special devotion to this or that saint as the Holy Spirit guides them, and this may lead them to pray daily to that saint. In a way I think All Saints Day, November 1st, is by far the most important saints' day, because it covers the vast multitude of saints who have not been canonised, and that will include good Christians whom we have known and who have now passed to the fuller life.

Indeed, in our devotion to the saints we should surely include the holy people we have known or with whom we are specially connected, like a saintly grandmother, whom we may never have met. She will, in my opinion, probably be doing far more praying for you than will a third century martyr from a distant land. I think the patterns of human relationship in this life are likely to be continued in a transformed way in the next one. So I ask for the prayers of the departed members of my family, as also of my monastic family and other departed people with some of whom I worked in a common ministry.

Catholics, or course, not only pray to the departed but also for the repose of their souls. The Administrator of Westminster Cathedral rightly wrote in the Westminster Record (August 1999) that people visit the tomb of the recently departed Cardinal Hume "and pray for the Cardinal and to the Cardinal". As to how much one prays for and how much to, I think we have to be led by the Holy Spirit. I personally normally pray daily for the repose of the souls of the departed members of my family, and I ask them to pray for me and for the other living members of my family. I feel that this really strengthens our bonds in the Communion of Saints.

I have also stuck on the wall above my bed pictures of departed people, a few of them canonised saints, some of them members of my family and of my monastic family, others of the holy people whom I knew and often worked with. I feel that in a general way I am united with them in prayer, until by the grace of God I am called to join them.

In general while Catholic-minded Christians pray for the departed, especially for departed members of the their families, Evangelical, Pentecostal and very liberal Christians do not. Catholics believe that they have a biblical backing for praying that the departed may rest in peace. In 2 Maccabees 12: 44-45: we read "For if he (Judas Maccabeus) were not expecting that those who had fallen would rise again, it would have been superfluous and foolish to pray for the dead. But if he was looking to the splendid reward that is laid up for those who fall asleep in godliness, it was a holy and pious thought. Therefore he made atonement for the dead, so that they might be delivered from their sin". For Catholics the books of Maccabees are part of the Old Testament, whereas for Protestants they are not - the Catholic Old Testament is larger than the Protestant one. (Some bibles include the book of Maccabees with a few other books under the title the Apocrypha). So Protestants unlike Catholics do not think that praying for the departed to rest in peace has a biblical basis.

Before I became a Catholic in 1945 I had never prayed for the repose of the departed. This has been for me a very beautiful and consoling practice ever since. After someone has died we can still help them with our prayers. We can also increase our union with them in Jesus through prayer. There is in addition the encouraging thought that when I depart I shall be accompanied by the prayers of others.

Following the pioneering lead of Dr Kenneth McAll, an Anglican Psychiatrist, I have for about 15 years been regularly celebrating Masses for the Healing of the Family Tree, sometimes referred to as Ancestral Masses. These are basically requiem Masses for deceased members of one's family and for other departed people with whom one has been linked. An increasing number of people seem to be finding these celebrations really helpful. Indeed, I myself am sometimes surprised at how helpful some people are finding them. And more and more priests are celebrating these Masses. I think that this area of the healing ministry will become more and more important in the years to come, especially in those countries where traditionally people have had a special concern for ancestors. For those interested, may I recommend Kenneth McAll's 'Healing of the Family Tree', Sheldon Press; 'Intergenerational Healing', by a Catholic priest, Robert de Grandis SSJ with Linda Schubert; 'From Generation to Generation', by Patricia A Smith, Jehovah Rapha Press ('highly' recommended by Francis MacNutt); 'Requiem Healing', by two Anglican Evangelical priests, Michael Mitton and Russ Parker, Darton, Longman and Todd. A Catholic Priest, John J Hampsch CMF, has a centre in the USA from which he distributes literature and tapes on the Healing of the Family Tree ministry, *(Claritian Tape Ministry, P O Box 19100, Los Angeles CA 90019).*

~~~~~~~~~

Catholic-minded Christians also ask the angels to help and protect them and others. Or they may prefer to ask God or Jesus to send angels to help and protect them.

In our liturgical calendar September 29th is the feast day of the Archangels Michael, Gabriel and Raphael, October 2nd is the feast day of our Guardian Angels. The Opening Prayer of the Mass of the Guardian Angels reads: "God our Father, in your loving providence you send your holy angels to watch over us. Hear our prayers, defend us always by their protection and let us share your life with them forever".

I do not want to repeat here things I wrote in my last book, 'I Saw Satan Fall, The Ways of Spiritual Warfare', in Appendix I 'Some Official Texts of the Catholic

Church on Angels and Demons', and in Appendix III, 'The Saints and Angels'. I felt rather sad when last week a television researcher or producer consulted me on the phone concerning a programme they were preparing on angels, which will obviously from what she said contain much on The New Age approach to angels. When I said that the Catholic Church believed in angels she seemed to doubt it, and said that she had been brought up a Catholic and that in her local church they had cut off all the angels wings with a saw! Christians should not hand over belief in angels to the New Age Movement, which exaggerates on this subject.

My belief in angels means more and more to me, and quite often I celebrate a votive Mass of the Guardian Angels. The thought that there is always at my side one of Jesus' angels, sent by Him to protect me, is a real source of comfort. My angel protects me spiritually, emotionally and physically. How many sins I might have committed, how many illness and accidents I might have had without angelic protection? Like many or most people I can remember a number of near misses in my life. Once when rock climbing on my own I had a very frightening and dangerous moment, once a very large bolder rolling down a hill missed the back of my head by inches, and more than once there have been close shaves with cars. Has my protection been just a matter of 'luck'. I do not think so. I think that often Jesus has been using His angels to keep me safe. That being so, it is surely right that I thank my guardian angel - or the angels in general - for all their help and protection. It is also right to ask the angels to protect us - and we can ask them also to protect other people, which is what Padre Pio did so frequently. I find myself chatting with my Guardian Angel at times, being grateful that he is there, and asking him to protect me, protect us, during this journey, this celebration, this ministry session, this difficult situation.

A friend of mine, who lives a very fruitful life for the Lord, has a seriously bad back problem, which has at times caused her leg to give-way unexpectedly, and this has resulted in some serious falls. Now whenever she leaves her home she calls on the angels to protect her in a special way. She also asks the angels to help her carry her shopping. This practice not only gives her more confidence, but, she is convinced has led to less falls and less serious falls. Perhaps her example and other things written here about angels may nudge or inspire some readers to think and pray more about angels. Ask the Holy Spirit to guide you in this matter.

If you prefer in prayer just to go direct to Jesus, or the heavenly Father, fine! It is all glory to Jesus or to the Father, Son and Holy Spirit in the end.

Appendix II
The Charismatic Renewal

Why have an appendix on the Charismatic Renewal in a book on prayer? Because the Charismatic Renewal and the Pentecostal Movement from which it sprang are in a special way movements of prayer, which in our times are affecting not only an increasing number of Christians but also an increasing proportion of Christians. Archbishop Paul Joseph Cordes, who was from 1981-96 the man officially appointed by Pope John Paul II as his link with the Catholic Charismatic Renewal, wrote in his book, 'A Call to Holiness. Reflections on the Catholic Charismatic Renewal' *(The Liturgical Press, Collegesville, Minnesota, 1997)*: "The Pentecostal Movement is considered to be 'the fastest growing missionary movement in the world. It is multiplying at a unique rate. A growth from zero to four hundred million in ninety years has never been experienced in the entire history of the Church.'" *(Page 1)* (The Archbishop is quoting the leading historian of the Pentecostal Movement, W J Hollenweger. The four hundred millions doubtless includes the Charismatic Renewal).

What can one say about the Charismatic Renewal in a relatively short Appendix? I am going to start autobiographically. In 1942 I had a conversion experience and was received into the Catholic Church. in 1946 I became a Benedictine monk, and in 1954 I was ordained priest. In 1972 I experienced what is normally called in the Charismatic Renewal the Baptism in the Holy Spirit or the Release of the Holy Spirit, and with it I received the Gift of Tongues. (see next Appendix). This experience of Baptism in the Holy Spirit was not another sacrament, it was not a first conversion to Jesus, it did not replace my monastic profession or my ordination to the priesthood, it did not make me less of a monk or a priest. On the contrary, it brought spiritual renewal to my monastic and priestly life. It also led to healing from depression.

Before my Baptism in the Holy Spirit I used to spend quite a lot of time in prayer daily, and the prayer felt meaningful and worthwhile. However, after that experience something was added. I felt that I knew Jesus in a new way. Somehow my life of prayer had become alive in a special way. I had especially a new freedom in praising and thanking Jesus, God. I had also a much greater faith in the power of prayer. It was after that experience of Baptism in the Holy Spirit that my charismatic healing ministry started. In fact 27 years later I regard that Baptism experience as an important turning point in my spiritual life.

Not that all my spiritual trials and failings were finished, not that I no longer needed to struggle against fears and anxieties, not that I was a better monk and priest than my monastic and priestly colleagues who had not had my kind of Baptism in the Holy Spirit experience and the Gift of Tongues. However, I am strongly convinced that since the 1972 experience I have, by the grace of God, been a better Christian - a less bad one - than I was before. I am also convinced that my life has been much more fruitful in helping others. Moreover, I became more open to the Holy Spirit and His gifts than I was before.

There are millions of Christians in the world today who would claim to have had a similar experience of the Baptism in the Holy Spirit to mine, although of course each of these experiences would be in a way unique - God blesses no two people in the same way. Sometimes this Baptism in the Holy Spirit experience will be separated in time from a first conversion, as happened to me. For many people, however, conversion and Baptism in the Holy Spirit coincide. For some people the Baptism in the Holy Spirit is a sudden experience, as happened to me. They can point to a precise date and a particular place. For other people this experience is a gradual process. They recognise that over the months or perhaps years a real change has happened in their spiritual life.

Recently I heard a lady telling how some years ago now she had been liberated from a very serious heroin addiction which was having disastrous consequences in her life - amongst other things she sold her mother's engagement ring and all her sister's jewels to get money for heroin. This lady was prayed over by a Catholic Charismatic prayer group. She had a wonderful experience of Jesus, was on cloud nine spiritually for several days, came off heroin without withdrawal symptoms, and never touched heroin again. Many people, however, who come to our prayer groups find that it is gradually that they are being spiritually transformed, but the gradual transformation may be no less deep than the sudden experience.

Now I must try to say more about this experience called the Baptism in the Holy Spirit or the Release of the

Holy Spirit, or the Outpouring of the Holy Spirit. I will describe this here in a Catholic perspective with which many other Christians would agree. As already said the Baptism in the Holy Spirit is not a sacrament. We Catholics believe, and many other Christians also, that Baptism properly administered to babies and other people is valid, and therefore cannot be repeated. However, it is evident that many Christians have been sacramentalised rather than evangelised. That is to say, that they have validly received the sacraments, but they have never really been brought to a living relationship with Jesus. This may in no way be their fault. For example, in an isolated village in South America which only sees a priest once a year, a person baptised as a baby may never have heard the gospel preached authentically, or have been truly instructed in the Christian faith.

The Holy Spirit received in Baptism and other sacraments may be tied up within us not only by ignorance, but also by worldliness, by tepidity and by sin. So the Holy Spirit may need to be released in our lives so that Jesus is free to take control in our lives as He wished to do. One way in which this can happen is when in a prayer group, normally after due preparation, someone is prayed with for the Release of or the Baptism in the Holy Spirit.

However, God can baptise someone in the Holy Spirit whenever and however He wills. For this to happen, obviously people do not have to have contact with the Charismatic Renewal or a Pentecostal Church. I have met numerous Christians from different churches whose lives are wonderfully full of the Holy Spirit without ever having had contact with the Charismatic Renewal or the Pentecostals. To start with, I personally think of holy monks and nuns, but then there are the not less holy and far more numerous holy married and single people in the world. And these holy people come from a variety of church backgrounds.

In a booklet, 'What Does Baptism in the Holy Spirit have to do with Christian Initiation', edited by Kilian McDonnell and George Montague for the Catholic Charismatic Renewal in 1991 *(The Liturgical Press, Collegeville)*, we read: "Baptism in the Holy Spirit is captive to no camp, whether liberal or conservative. Nor is it identified with any one movement, nor with one style of prayer, worship or community. On the contrary, we believe that this gift of the baptism in the Holy Spirit belongs to the Christian inheritance of all those sacramentally initiated into the church." *(page 10)*.

Archbishop Cordes writes in the book cited earlier: "Baptism in the Holy Spirit is a concrete experience of the 'Grace of Pentecost', in which the working of the Holy Spirit becomes an experienced reality in the life of the individual and of the faith community". *(page 11)* He goes on to write "that 'Baptism in the Spirit' is a free and unmerited gift of God and is usually the fruit of a free decision, a step of conversion, an act of entrusting everything to Christ the Lord, of giving one's whole life to Him so that He might transform it. It is also the decision to surrender to the Holy Spirit, without setting any limits on divine free action, a decision to receive in faith the fullness of God's grace". *(pages 13 - 14)*.

All Christians are called to holiness. As the second Vatican Council has said: "All the faithful of Christ of whatever rank or status are called to the fullness of the Christian life and the perfection of charity" *(Lumen Gentium 20)*. And it is the same holiness: "one and the same holiness is cultivated by all who are moved by the Spirit of God and who obey the voice of the Father, worshipping the Father in Spirit and truth" *(Lumen Gentium 41)*.

So what is special about the Charismatic Renewal and its worship? The answer is clearly not that one needs to go to Charismatic Prayer groups or churches to receive the Baptism in the Holy Spirit. Christians are receiving the Baptism of the Holy Spirit in Carmelite convents, in the Focolare movement, in parishes, in families, and in every Christian denomination and community. The Holy Spirit blows where and when He wills. However, it does seem that in our times charismatic groups and churches are being used by God in a special way to bring many people to the grace of conversion and of Baptism in the Holy Spirit. The rapid growth of the Pentecostal and Charismatic churches and groups would seem to confirm this.

Can one speak of a charismatic spirituality? I think one can, but with variations. I have been participating in charismatic prayer meetings and services for twenty seven years, and meeting the people involved in them, who come from different church backgrounds, and different countries. One recognises certain common characteristics and certain common experiences. So I have in a way felt truly at home in Anglican charismatic services such as those at Holy Trinity, Brompton and St Andrew's in Chorley Wood; in a charismatic prayer group or service in a Pentecostal church; in a nondenominational fellowship (House Church), in a black charismatic church, and in other charismatic traditions.

What are the characteristics of this charismatic spirituality? I would say:

(1) A living personal relationship with Jesus, so that in a real way we know Jesus and not only about Him.

(2) A personal experience of the Holy Spirit, and His working in our lives.

(3) The release of praise and thanksgiving in our life of prayer.

(4) Confidence in the power of prayer and a serious life of intercession.

(5) Learning to listen to Jesus, God.

(6) Spending enough time in prayer. When Christians get involved in the Charismatic Renewal they normally spend considerably more time in prayer.

(7) A love for the Bible and the practice of reading it prayerfully.

(8) Catholics who become involved in the Charismatic Renewal normally find that the Eucharist means more to them, as also the other sacraments and devotion to Mary.

(9) A concern for evangelisation and actually doing more to spread the Gospel.

(10) A desire to grow in the gifts of the Holy Spirit. These gifts would include for the group as a whole, the gifts of Tongues, Prophecy and Healing, in order to serve Christ's Kingdom more fruitfully.

(11) The practice of some fasting from food and drink,

health permitting.

(12)   Seeking to build up Christian community, which of course covers a wide range of activities.

One could object that most of the above points apply to any sound Christian spiritually. Very true. The last thing I would want to do is to claim monopolies for the Charismatic Renewal. Indeed some of the above characteristics may normally be more in evidence in other spiritualities, for example, Bible reading in the Neo-Catechuminate, and in some evangelical groups. Let us thank God for the workings of the Holy Spirit wherever they are to be found!

I think something more needs to be said here about the gifts or charisms of the Holy Spirit. As Archbishop Cordes wrote in his book "A Call to Holiness" referred to earlier: "As fruits of Pentecost, charisms have never been absent from the life of the Church. The twentieth century has seen, through a new and intense Outpouring of the Holy Spirit, also a new and more intense experience of these charisms among God's people in order to minister more adequately to the needs of our time". *(page 42)*

One charism which seems to be especially linked with the Charismatic Renewal is the gift of healing mentioned twice by St Paul in I Corinthians 14. Of course spiritual and emotional healing is happening in every authentic Christian community. And physical healings in answer to prayer are happening in Christian communities which are not linked with the Charismatic Renewal. I know a Catholic layman who knew nothing about the Charismatic Renewal when he found God using him to do remarkable healings, including important physical ones. However, it does seem to me that in general the gift of healing and the healing ministry of prayer are considerably more flourishing in the Charismatic Renewal and the Pentecostal churches than elsewhere in the Christian world. And I find myself asking whether it is right that some churches and Christian groups encourage and fruitfully use the charism of healing and others do not. Are not the sick and suffering Christians in the second group missing out on something which should normally be an integral part of the Christian community?

There are also the charisms directly connected with evangelisation. It seems to be usually the Pentecostal and Charismatic churches and groups which are most specially concerned with, and effective in, evangelising unbelievers, and because of this they are in many places the growing section of Christianity. Where are the 'evangelists' *(Ephesians 4.11)* in some Christian communities? Think of the amazing fruitfulness of the Alpha course in prisons and elsewhere, which of course comes from an Anglican charismatic church, Holy Trinity, Brompton. There is also, for example, the large number of converts to Christianity coming in these years from the outreach of Catholics involved in the Charismatic Renewal in Uganda.

If we look at the history of spirituality in the Christian church we find that there have been at times special movements of the Holy Spirit giving rise to characteristic spiritualities. In the 4th and 5th centuries, for example, many men and women went out into the desert of the Middle East as monks and nuns, and they followed their own kind of spirituality, which included saying large numbers of psalms and fasting. Another example would be the spiritual school of the Franciscans, with a stress on holy poverty. On the Reformation side there was, for example, John and Charles Wesley and their followers, with the rich tradition of hymn singing. Also in this country there was the famous Welsh revival at the beginning of this century. Among Catholics there was the spirituality centred round devotion to the Sacred Heart of Jesus.

In all these examples there were large numbers of people caught up in a common spirituality, sharing to some degree in a common spiritual experience which was the work of the Holy Spirit. I think this is happening to some extent in our times with the Pentecostal-Charismatic movement. I have been to Pentecostal-Charismatic services and prayer groups in different churches and in different counties, and I find the Holy Spirit doing the same sort of things in largely the same way. For example, receiving the gift of tongues is basically the same among Pentecostals and Catholic Charismatics, as also being healed by the laying on of hands. And there is a largely shared pool of Charismatic hymns and songs coming from Charismatic sources, which, incidentally, has largely spread to other Christian traditions.

Of course there are also differences. My own spiritual life is centred round the daily celebration of the Eucharist, which would not be the case for a Pentecostal. However, I feel that I have a very real spiritual link with the Pentecostals, and this link is ecumenically important. Pope John Paul II said in an address to leaders of the

Catholic Charismatic Renewal on May 7th 1981: "By your experience of the many gifts of the Holy Spirit which are shared also with our separated brothers and sisters, yours is the special joy of growing in a desire for the unity to which the Spirit guides us and in a commitment to the serious task of ecumenism". Yes, the Catholic Charismatic Renewal has a special ecumenical vocation which, I think, nothing else can replace.

Have the Pentecostal movement and the Charismatic Renewal their own special dangers and temptations? Perhaps I can list a few areas where there can be difficulties:

(1)   Strong charismatic personalities can become self-seeking and lead others astray.

(2)   Charismatics can suffer from spiritual pride and think themselves better than other Christians. (In my experience it is normally not so much a question of charismatics thinking that they are better than other Christians, but of other Christians thinking that is what charismatics think!).

(3)   If there can be true prophecy, then there can also be false prophecy, which sometimes happens.

(4)   Things can go wrong in the healing ministry and in the deliverance ministry.

(5)   There can be indiscreet evangelisation.

(6)   There can be an anti-intellectual attitude, less common now than in the past.

(7)   There can be an anti-ecumenical attitude, linked with exaggerated criticism of other Christians.

(8)   There can be a too narrow attitude as to who is saved by Jesus.

(9)   There can be a neglect of social problems, and a lack of concern about the environment, this last surely a common failing of many Christians.

(10)   There can be an exaggerated emotionalism.

However, many of the above difficulties are found in other churches, and all Christian traditions can have their own special problems. For example, in the Catholic Church we can suffer from clericalism, and liberal Protestants can compromise over the teaching of Jesus and the Bible, and the Eastern Orthodox Christians can be ecumenically very negative.

Does God want every Christian to become involved in the Charismatic Renewal? As I explained earlier, He wants every Christian to receive the Baptism in the Spirit. But I do not think He wants every Christian to become involved in the Charismatic Renewal, in the sense of joining a charismatic church or group. Apart from the fact that there may be no charismatic groups near them, some Christians are put off by charismatic worship and do not feel it is the right thing for them. Furthermore, if someone is very happy with the Christian support they are receiving in, say, the Neo-Catechuminate, or their local Anglican church, or in a Benedictine monastery, God may well not wish them to go to a charismatic group.

However, I must add that quite a number of the leaders of the Catholic Charismatic Renewal started by feeling very negative towards it, and then God greatly blessed them through the Charismatic Renewal. There is certainly something new in the ethos of charismatic worship which some people can find off-putting, even frightening, especially in the beginning. A lady told me that she had gone once to our large prayer meeting and felt she had to run out - she said she felt there was too much 'electricity'. I asked her if it was good 'electricity'. She replied without hesitation, "Oh, yes". But she never came back! Some people find charismatic worship too emotional, but may be in some cases precisely what they need is for Jesus to touch their emotions - He came to heal and transform every aspect of our lives, including our emotions. Some Christian groups can give the impression that they are God's frozen people, not His chosen people.

In every Christian tradition there have been regrettable cases and events, but taking all in all the positive fruits of the Charismatic Renewal surely far outweigh the negative. If it were not so Pope Paul VI and Pope John Paul II would not have given the Charismatic Renewal the warm welcome and encouragement which they have done. For instance, the present Pope speaking to leaders of the Catholic Charismatic Renewal on March 14th 1992 said: "As you celebrate the twenty-fifth anniversary of the beginning of the Catholic Charismatic Renewal, I willingly join you in giving praise to God for the many fruits which it has borne in the life of the Church. The emergence of the Renewal following the Second Vatican Council was a particular gift of the Holy Spirit to the Church. It was a sign of a desire on the part of many Catholics to live more fully their baptismal dignity and vocation as adopted sons and daughters of the Father, to know the redeeming power of Christ our Saviour in a more intense experience of individual and group prayer, and to follow the teaching of the Scriptures by reading them in the light of the same Spirit who inspired their writing.

Certainly one of the most important results of this spiritual re-awakening has been that increased thirst for holiness which is seen in the lives of individuals and in the whole Church".

In matters of religion many Christians tend to be conservative and do not like changes. Remember the large number of Catholics who got upset after Vatican II when the altars were changed round for Mass, but now they are happy with it. Understandably many Christians feel ill at ease with the new ethos of charismatic worship when they first experience it. May I plead that people do not say too easily and too quickly, "This is not for me". Perhaps it is *not* for you, but perhaps it may be; as many Catholics and other Christians have found after persevering for a time. Perhaps you need the healing ministry which the Charismatic Renewal offers. Perhaps your prayer life or your Christian life as a whole has grown stale. Perhaps God is wanting to give you something through the Charismatic Renewal. Pray about it!

Appendix III
The Gift of Tongues

For this appendix on the Gift of Tongues, I am reproducing the section on this subject which I wrote in a Catholic Truth Society booklet 'The Catholic Charismatic Renewal' *(1992)*. The booklet had a Forward by Bishop Ambrose Griffiths OSB.

"The Gift of Tongues (Glossolalia)

The gift of tongues or glossolalia is for many people the most special characteristic of the Pentecostal-Charismatic Renewal - as also the most puzzling characteristic. Is the so-called speaking in tongues anything more than giving way to gibberish? Is not speaking in tongues an emotional excess which discredits Christianity for non-believers? What is the purpose of speaking in tongues when the great majority of Christians have found their own language (or Latin) quite adequate for use in prayer?

The first thing to note is that the gift of tongues or glossolalia has a firm basis in the New Testament. In Mark 16:17 we read that Jesus said that believers 'will speak in new tongues'. We find this happening on the day of Pentecost: "All of them were filled with the Holy Spirit and began to speak in other languages, as the Spirit gave them ability' *(Acts 2:4)*. It happened in the house of Cornelius: 'While Peter was still speaking, the Holy Spirit fell upon all who heard the word. The circumcised believers who had come with Peter were astounded that the gift of the Holy Spirit had been poured on the Gentiles, for they heard them speaking in tongues and extolling God' *(Acts 10:44).* It also happened at Ephesus: 'When Paul had laid his hands on them, the Holy Spirit came upon them, and they spoke in tongues and prophesied - altogether there were about twelve of them' *(Acts 19:6).* Twice in I Corinthians chapter 12 Paul refers to 'various kinds of tongues' as a gift of the Holy Spirit. In I Corinthians chapter 14, where Paul is in part correcting certain abuses of the gift of tongues in Corinth and expressing his preference in general for the gift of prophecy, he nevertheless says: 'Now I would like all of you to speak in tongues,' and 'I thank God that I speak in tongues more than all of you.'

In addition to the biblical evidence there is the fact that many millions of Christians in the world today, including many Catholics, claim that they have received the gift of tongues and that this gift has truly deepened their prayer life. This claim is made by bishops and learned theologians as also by people who cannot read and children under ten. In the face of so much evidence it is surely difficult to deny that very many Christians, including large numbers of Catholics, have been spiritually helped by receiving the gift of tongues. Some years ago it was estimated that at least 700,000 Catholics in the USA prayed in tongues, so it will be seen that this is not a rare gift for just a few people.

The gift of tongues is mainly a gift which helps people to pray better especially to praise better. It is also helpful for intercession, especially when someone does not know what to pray for *(Romans 8:26).* Paul in I Corinthians 14:4 writes: "Those who speak in a tongue, build up themselves." Less often, however this gift in conjunction with the gift of interpretation of tongues (*I Corinthians 12:10)* is used for giving messages, in a similar way to the gift of prophecy.

The gift of tongues is not to be thought of as preaching the gospel to or communicating with people who do not know your own language - that experience was a special grace for the day of Pentecost itself, although it seems that it still happens on very rare occasions. Catholic theologians involved in the Charismatic Renewal do not believe that in general the authentic gift of tongues involves actually speaking in a language that is or has been spoken by human beings. However, there is something language-like about the authentic gift of tongues which distinguishes it from mere gibberish - it sounds like a language in a way that gibberish does not. Linguistic experts can tell the difference between the authentic gift of tongues and someone just mouthing gibberish.

The gift of tongues is not ecstacy; speaking in tongues does not involve going into an ecstasy. I can decide to speak in tongues just as easily as deciding to speak in English - and I can pray in tongues just as badly as I can pray in English, for example, when I am distracted.

The gift of tongues is not to be thought of as a sign of sanctity or as a very high spiritual gift. Doubtless some people are given the gift of tongues not because they are good at praying but because they are not good at it and are in real need of help in the prayer life. However, the gift of tongues is normally an aid to contemplation.

Jackie Pullinger, an English woman with a very powerful spiritual ministry in Hong Kong, is sometimes used to bring the gift of tongues to very new converts who do not yet even know the Our Father. She is also used to getting heroin addicts off heroin without withdrawal symptoms through the gift of tongues. Tongues can be a very powerful gift!

It is not necessary to speak in tongues in order to receive the Baptism in the Holy Spirit. I know Catholics who have clearly received the Baptism in the Holy Spirit and powerful spiritual gifts of healing and prophecy, yet who do not pray in tongues. However, the gift of tongues normally comes sooner or later to Christians involved in the Charismatic Renewal. And the gift of tongues seems often to be the gateway leading to other gifts. Not a few Catholics going to charismatic prayer meetings start by saying strongly that they do not want to receive the gift of tongues, even though they like other aspects of the prayer meeting. With time this negative attitude normally fades away, until the day comes when they ask to be prayed with for the gift of tongues - and they usually receive it. Some Catholics tend to be over-cerebral in the field of the conscious intellect - indeed they tend to be afraid of all religious experience. Such Catholics may find the gift of tongues difficult, but perhaps it would be a real help to them, for it could give them greater spiritual freedom. There is a sense in which we have to be willing to become a fool for Christ's sake, and for some people this can apply to receiving the gift of tongues.

Much that I have written here will seem very bewildering to many readers. Let me assure them that when I first heard someone praying in tongues I myself was most suspicious and highly sceptical. However, I was won over when I first heard many people in a large gathering singing in tongues, and this has been a sign to many other people also. Sometimes at a charismatic gathering for worship, people will start singing in tongues together, and this can create a very beautiful harmonious and spiritually uplifting sound which no scientist can explain. There is no human conductor, no fixed words, no fixed music, no preparations beforehand, yet instead of being total chaos it can be very inspiring spiritually, a sign that the Holy Spirit is at work in the gift of tongues. I can only say, go and experience it for yourself!"

I received the Gift of Tongues in 1972, and this gift means more and more to me as the years go by. I pray in tongues a number of times every day. I am sure that my prayer life, like that of millions of other Christians, has been greatly enriched by this gift. However, I am equally sure that many Christians who do not have the Gift of Tongues are certainly better prayers than I am.

Should some readers wonder whether God wants them to receive this gift, pray about it. If you feel that He does, ask the Holy Spirit to give you this gift. You should probably also go to some charismatic church or prayer group and ask them to pray with you for the gift, to the Glory of the Father, from whom all good things come.

Further copies of this book can be obtained from:

www.goodnewsbooks.net

or by post from:

Goodnews Books & Audio
60 Wickstead Avenue
Luton, Beds. LU4 9DP
Tel: 01582 571011
email: orders@goodnewsbooks.net

Other books by Dom Benedict Heron,
also obtainable from Goodnews Books:

"I Saw Satan Fall", the ways of spiritual warfare
Praying for Healing, the challenge

In my dream the whole side of this mountain was under construction. We (my SD school, w/ Ann driving) was returning to school — or just driving along over what had been the road + was now in upheaval. We seemed to be fine — Ann kept driving. The mountain is all unsettled.